I Always Sang for My Father

or anyone who would listen

I
Always
Sang for
My Father

or anyone who would listen

◆

Victor Tedesco

WITH TRUDI HAHN

SYREN BOOK COMPANY
MINNEAPOLIS

Most Syren Books are available at special quantity discounts for bulk purchases for sales promotions, premiums, fund-raising, and educational needs. For details, write

Syren Book Company
Special Sales Department
5120 Cedar Lake Road
Minneapolis, MN 55416

Published by
Syren Book Company
5120 Cedar Lake Road
Minneapolis, MN 55416

Printed in the United States of America on acid-free paper

ISBN-13: 978-0-929636-55-9
ISBN-10: 0-929636-55-4

LCCN 2005936040

Cover design by Kyle G. Hunter
Book design by Wendy Holdman

Cover: The modern-day Vic Tedesco big band played in 1986 at the Roof Garden of Hamm's Brewery in Saint Paul with yours truly out front.

To order additional copies of this book see the form at the back of this book or go to www.itascabooks.com

Contents

Part II—The Stateside War

Part III—Radio Days

Part IV—People-Pleasing Politics

Part V—Retiring to Music

Acknowledgments

A lifetime of memories can't be recorded without some prompting from other folks. People who helped with details in this book include Don Boxmeyer, Mary Gentile, Leonard Levine, Georgia DeCoster Lindeke, Dennis McGrath, John Ricci, Jane Shanard, Arlene Scheunemann, Mike Sirian, Peggy Torgenson, and Linda Vasquez.

Foreword

I had a wonderful childhood filled with music, encouraged by my mother and father. Songs and records and my own big band have filled my life with music to this day.

In 1970, a movie called "I Never Sang for My Father" was released, starring Melvyn Douglas and Gene Hackman. Hackman's character had a terrible time with his father, played by Douglas. There was no harmony.

I was fortunate in my own life that my father and I loved each other. I always sang for him. So I named my book *I Always Sang for My Father* to honor those parents who love and encourage their children.

Vic Tedesco
Saint Paul, Minnesota
August 2005

Bunky and FeeFee and Hamfat, Oh My

The late Gentilly Yarusso wrote an unpublished manuscript about Swede Hollow and gave away hundreds of copies. It included a list of the fun nicknames we "Railroad Islanders" gave to each other. To my knowledge, these nicknames were never considered or intended to be insulting or derogatory.

THE LADIES:

Marion (Sarracco) Bucci	Mar
Marie (Policano) Capra	Babe
Margaret (Dinzeo) McQuade	Mugs
Amelia (Dinzeo) Sockness	Melsie

THE GENTS:

Armando Anzevino	Ole
Dominic Barilla	Deano
Richard Biagini	Coke
Philip Bifulk	Cheechat
Albert Blasiola	BaBa
Dominic Caliguire	Bunky
James Caliguire	Weazel
Albert Colyard	Hotfeet
Carl Connie	DonGeech
Dominic Controneo	Raji (Little Raji)
Rocco Costello	Wop
Dominic Crea	Raji (Big Raji)
Joseph Crea	Peppy

Tony Crea	Todo
Louis Cucchiarella	GeeGee
Nick Cucchiarella	Bishop
Pat Cucchiarella	Pucka
Ralph Cucchiarella	Buffet
John Deloia	Rabbits
Carl DeMike	Allu, Congo Coke
Angelo DePalma	Cookie
Tony Destasio	Two Ton
Bob Facente	Bama
Ernie Ferrozzo	Tarblock
Louis Frascone	Spoco
Victor Frascone	Slits
Gene Frisco	Professor
David Gagliardi	Banjo Eyes
Emil Gatto	Eightball
Dominc Genova	Ambrose
Frank Genova	Sharkey
William Gentile	Willy
Rocco Legato	Wop
Joe Madia	Flossy
Joe Mancuso	Sheriff
Albert Mangine	Turk
Julio Mangine	Jolly
Tony Mangine*	Champ
Tony Mangine*	Tumbo
John Mastrofrancesco	Irish, Dusty
Tom Media	Pissi-pisoni
Romolo Mondo	Johncracker
Americo Montanari	Chippy Chop
George Morelli	Butch
Mariano Morelli	Buddy Taylor

*Two different boys.

Floyd Orlando	Flutie-pee-peep
Danny Orsello	Floppy
Frank Paloney	Cheech
Gerald Paloney	FeeFee
Jim Palumbo	Pasta Shoot
George Pangal	King Kong
Joe Pariana	Windy
Ralph Pariana	Otta
Patrick Pilla	Eagle Beak
Tony Pilla	Red
Angelo Policano	Chief
John Policano	Uncle John
Tom Policano	Balsie
William Polo	Hamfat
John Raiola	Baldy
Louis Raiola	Juicy
Marvin Raiola	Honey
Pat Ricci	Blackie
Carmen Ricci	Harbor Lights
Frank Ricci*	Medigan
Frank Ricci*	Cocky
John Ricci	Gaspipe
Richard Richie	Ace
Mike Sirian	Kiki
Al Sarracco	Mickey Rat
Carmen Sarracco	Chief Wahoo
Carmen Sarrack	Curly Carlson
Nick Savino	Garbo
Angelo Scalze	Wildcat Eddie Mason
Carl Scalze	Skinny
Ralph Scalze	Fatty
Tommy Sirian	Eleven Round

*Two different boys.

Joe Skipon	Skippy
Sam Skipon	Artzon
Louis Spelious	Yokum
Mike Sylvester	Slinger Mike
John Tarlizzo	Fats
Victor Tedesco	Vic Tedoo
Al Tinucci	Cowboy
Joe Venaglia	Vinegar
Louis Venaglia	Bib
Angie Vitali	Six Gun
Armondo Yarusso	Dumbbox
Danny Yarusso	Murphy
David Yarusso	Dial
Gentile Yarusso	Gindy
Joe Yarusso	Chili Joe
Lawrence Yarusso	Zeke
Joe Yekaldo	Cosum

Dedication

I would like to dedicate this book to my family:

My wife, Florence;
my son Tony;
my daughter Patricia;
my grandchildren Justin and Kirstin,
and my late daughter Elizabeth.

Vic Tedesco

PART ONE

Up from Swede Hollow

CHAPTER 1

The Wood in My Family Tree Is Italian

THEY THREW HIM OVERBOARD—he was dead. My grandfather, Vittorio Zamboni, died of pneumonia at sea when he was returning to America after a visit to the old country to settle a family argument.

He had come to Brooklyn in 1904 to seek his fortune, but it was misfortune that took him back to Italy in 1906. Back home in Cotronei, the family wanted the former policeman to settle a dispute over who owned a certain sewing machine, a valuable possession.

Vittorio had been born in Venice on Sept. 10, 1862. He joined the Italian army in 1883, the year he turned 21. After an honorable discharge, he joined the police in Rome.

He had a good reputation, so when a bandit started stealing pigs in the Calabrian village of Cotronei, where a pig was worth a lot of money, Vittorio

My grandfather, Vittorio Zamboni, in the uniform of the police of Rome, in the late 1880s.

3

was designated as the police officer to go to Calabria to catch the culprit. It was said if anyone could catch the pig stealer, Vittorio Zamboni could. And he did.

He also caught love. In Cotronei he met and married my grandmother Maria, who was from Spain. (Nobody remembers why she was in Italy.) Vittorio was an extremely handsome man, and many of the women in the village were after him, but he said he loved his little Maria. He also loved to sing operatic arias, and each of the six children born to the couple were given operatic names: Aïda (my mother), Elenora, Esther, Travatore, Traviate and Dante.

Of the six, only my mother, Aïda, born Aug. 18, 1895, and her older sister Elenora were alive in 1906 when the sewing-machine quarrel brought Vittorio back to Cotronei. Then he took sail back to America and died aboard ship. With no refrigeration available, the only choice for the ship's crew was to bury him at sea when the pneumonia took him. The outcome of the dispute vanished from my family's history when he went under the waves.

The news of his death broke my grandmother's heart, and she died shortly thereafter. Elenora was 17 and married. Aïda, only 11, went to live with her sister and her husband at their home in Cotronei. When Aïda was 17, she married a lad of Cotronei, Antonio Tedesco.

Antonio's father, Bernardo Nicola Tedesco, didn't have as exciting a life as my mother's father, Vittorio Zamboni. Bernardo, a quiet, unassuming man, had a little land, was self-supporting and kept to himself. He was a little guy like my dad, only 5 feet, 4 inches tall. He married Serafina Pariana, a woman of strong personality who dominated him, and they lived their entire lives in Cotronei.

My father, Antonio Tedesco, was born Sept. 13, 1888, the youngest of five children. He was the only one who lived to adulthood. His twin brother, Giovanni, another brother, Savario, and two sisters, Francesca and Elizabeth, all died young.

Antonio married Aïda in 1912. He was a shoe repairman, a

respected position in Cotronei, but after their first child, my brother Nicola, was born in 1913, Antonio wanted to emigrate to America for a better life. He couldn't afford to take his wife and son with him, so he set out alone, not knowing that Aïda was pregnant again. She gave birth to a little girl, Serafina, after he had left. Serafina didn't get to find out whether life truly would be better for the family in America. She died at the age of three months in 1914.

CHAPTER 2

Up from Swede Hollow

Antonio was 25 when he sailed away from Aïda on the Regina D'Italia, leaving behind his friends and family among the 1,400 residents of Cotronei. He arrived on April 3, 1914, at the bustling Ellis Island immigration center in New York. He started his life in America in Brooklyn, where repairing shoes didn't carry the same respect it had in Italy. But he worked, saved money, and eventually came west with Joseph Bruno of Sicily, who lived in the same boarding house. They moved to Saint Paul. (Please note—I never abbreviate the word "saint." 'Tis a pet peeve of mine.)

My father was proud to be an American. He went to night school to learn to speak English—something every new citizen should make a number one priority, in my opinion. By 1921, seven years after arriving in America, he could afford to send for Aïda and Nicola.

Aïda was very reluctant to leave Italy, afraid of what the future would bring, but my father was adamant about her coming.

Most of Antonio's friends from the small village of Cotronei had emigrated to Saint Paul. So had his cousin, Nicola Pariana. Nicola and his wife, Conchetta, and their children were already living in Swede Hollow when Aïda and son Nicola arrived—after they got a little lost.

Aïda and her son, known in America as Nicholas, didn't speak English, so she had a piece of paper pinned to her clothing to notify the train conductor that she and Nick were to get off in Saint Paul. The conductor slipped up and they ended up in

Minneapolis. The conductor was mad. He said, "Goddamn son of a bitch," and had to take them back to Saint Paul.

There my brother Nick, age eight, greeted my father. He wanted to impress him with the English he had learned, so he said, "Goddamn son of a bitch." My dad slapped him and said that was a bad word.

And so they settled down in Swede Hollow.

It was the poorest section in the city. The Swedes who had settled the area in the early 1800s dominated until about 1900, when the Italians started moving in, many of them from my parents' province of Calabria.

Antonio and Aïda and their son lived in a spartan house—no running water, so the bathroom was an outhouse, but they did have electricity for lights. A lot of wood was stored in the house, a safe distance from the wood stove. The stove provided heat, and Aïda cooked on it as well.

I, Victor John Tedesco, was born May 22, 1922, in the back bedroom with a midwife in attendance and a bureau drawer for a crib. My sister, Mary, followed on Aug. 7, 1923. The next year the family moved from the Hollow to the city market area, where my brother Albert was born at home in 1925.

It was another "high class" neighborhood inhabited by Jews and Italians. We lived in a fourplex at the corner of Norris and Canada Streets, next to Brinkman's Junkyard. Two blocks away was the city market, which covered about six blocks by three blocks. Farmers from up to 50 miles away rumbled in with their trucks loaded with fruits and vegetables. For a short while, when I was about eight, I worked there, helping farmers set up their stands. We had moonshiners, too, three or four who became respectable businessmen after Prohibition ended in 1933. One of them, John Degideo, boasts about his bootlegging days on the menu at his popular West Seventh Street restaurant, Degideo's.

Around us in the close-knit community lived many Italian families, like the family of Joseph Bruno from Sicily; the man who had come west with my father was my godfather when I made my confirmation. The Dagostinos were Calabrese. The

Biagis, who were Tuscans and generally felt they were better than the southern Italians, were the last Italian family to leave the city market area. Their house was close to Saint Mary's Catholic Church and School. The Danas, who had a grocery store one block away at Grove and Canada, were considered well off. These families remained in the city market area for quite a long time. Tony Pangel, Gabriel Mancuso and the Taruccios were from Cotronei. They had played together as children in Calabria. Now, as adults, they were united in Little Italy in Saint Paul.

In 1926 my dad bought a house on Collins Street. It was about three miles east of Norris and Canada Streets, and only two blocks west of Swede Hollow. Now we were in the heart of Little Italy.

CHAPTER 3

Spaghetti Twice a Week

Gᴿᴏᴡɪɴɢ ᴜᴘ ɪɴ Lɪᴛᴛʟᴇ Iᴛᴀʟʏ was a complete joy. Collins Street was noisy, with a lot of traffic, and I loved the noise. I'd fall asleep at night listening to the rumble of the trucks driving by and the whistle of the trains passing underneath the Lafayette Street bridge—unless I was staying up reading comic books under the sheets in bed, flashlight in hand.

The Collins Street house was not in the best of shape. Dad paid $1,200 for it—cheap even in 1926. But my brother Nick was very handy, and already 13. He spent many hours putting the house in tip-top shape. He put a nice new front porch on the house. He put new windows in, painted the house inside and out. It was quite a job for a 13-year-old, but he grew up real quick. In fact, when Nick was finished, it was one of the nicest houses in the neighborhood. He was a perfectionist. You'd never want to hire him by the hour. He wouldn't settle for inferior work.

My sister Mary, who was 14 months younger than me, was the

At the house on Collins Street in Saint Paul, about 1928: My mother, Aïda, with my sister, Mary, at left; brother, Albert, known as Babe, and me, Vic, about six years old.

9

only girl in the family. Our sister Serafina had died in Cotronei at the age of three months. Brother Albert and I played together a lot because we were only four years apart in age.

My dad was a small man, but only in size. His name was Antonio, but everyone called him "Sam, the *scarpara*." *Scarpara* means shoemaker. I don't know where "Sam" came from.

About 5 feet tall, he loved to play bocce ball and was one of, if not the most popular guy in the neighborhood. He was always invited to house parties in Little Italy to entertain his friends.

He played guitar and trombone. He seemed to favor the guitar as he could accompany his vocalizing. He would play guitar and sing around the house, too. Sometimes a young Mexican man, Peter Davora, would come to our house and sing with my dad accompanying on guitar.

Ours was a happy home. Our family didn't have much money but we were rich when it came to togetherness, respect, love and faith in God.

In the winter, we would all sit around the kitchen wood stove, roast chestnuts and take turns telling stories. We closed up the two back rooms to conserve heat and used only four rooms—kitchen, living room, parents' bedroom and the dining room, where we three kids slept.

Dad was a prankster. We would be at the dinner table and he would say to my mom in Italian, "Look at the mosquito on the ceiling." She would look up and see nothing. In the meantime, he would lift her choice piece of melon from her plate and was devouring it. I think my mom went along with the gag just to make him feel good, and to make sure that we would all get a good laugh.

In the winter, two back rooms were closed up to conserve heat, and we three youngest slept in the dining room. From left, Mary, Albert and Vic.

My mother used to sing to me Italian songs such as "Santa Lucia," "Funiculi, Funicula," and "Torno a Surriento." She had a beautiful voice. She must have got that treasure from her father, Vittorio Zamboni, the operatic tenor. She wanted to teach me all the songs in Italian, but I didn't want to listen. To this day I regret it.

My mother never did learn to speak fluent English. She would talk to us in Italian—my parents always called me Vittorio—and we would talk to her in English and it worked out OK. Mary and Nick could speak fluent Italian.

Aïda was a great cook, limited mostly to Italian cuisine. She made everything from scratch, basically potatoes prepared in many different ways, and spaghetti every Thursday and Sunday like clockwork.

I didn't have any canned goods to eat until I was 12, when, unbeknownst to my ma, I ate some canned corn. I'm not sure where it came from. I know I didn't buy it and I didn't steal it. Maybe I found it in a broken case along the railroad tracks. Anyhow, I opened the can, heated the corn still in the can on a campfire in my backyard, and ate it in my little shack.

The shack was a wooden box, about 3 feet by 4 feet by 4 feet high, that I found down by the tracks. The wood was heavy, so a couple of us picked it up and put it on a wagon to haul it up to the backyard of the house. It was Joe and Lawrence Venaglia from next door who helped, so the three of us shared it.

The shack was with us for only one summer. We played in it every day. But when winter came, my dad dismantled it and we had firewood for a day or two.

I kissed my first girl in that little shack. She lived next door and is still with us, so I'm not going to tell you who she was. She was beautiful then and still is.

CHAPTER 4

Hot Dagos and Cold Ice

COLLINS STREET WAS A MIX of residential dwellings and small businesses. Starting on the eastern end of the three-block-long street was Morelli's grocery store. It was small, not the supermarket it is today, run by the third generation, Jimmy and Louie Morelli. Up the block was Russo's grocery and at the western edge of the street was Machovec's grocery, Leonard's Bar and another business. Leonard's became Mike's Pin-Up Bar, which earned the reputation of having the best hot dago sandwich in town.

We kids used to hang out in Russo's, especially in the winter. The older boys—teenagers, early 20s—always had a wager on something. One time they wanted to see who could consume the most raw eggs in beer, or maybe it was water. I think the top number was 20. I'll wager the winner didn't feel too good.

Next to Russo's was the Crispus Attucks home, a combined orphanage and old folks' home for black people, who weren't allowed to live with white folks at rest homes, as they were called then. We kids got along just fine with them. We'd go up and sit on the porch and talk with them. It was a pleasure to have conversations with them—great rapport. One thing we didn't do, was to have prejudice. We didn't even know the word!

CHAPTER 5

The Neighbors Sold
Almost Anything

Russo sold his store to Sam Gellerman. He was more aggressive as a businessman. We kids delivered handbills advertising his store. I hate to tell you how many ended up in the sewer—so I won't.

We kids weren't always angels. Joe the ice man always got mad at us when we called him "Fatty Joe." He was no taller than 5 feet and weighed at least 250 pounds. He could have been anywhere between 50 and 75 years old—when you're a kid, everyone older than 30 was old.

Joe was single and boarded with the Orsello family on North Street. His ice wagon was a handcart on two big wheels with a good-size wooden box on it. He sold small blocks of ice from door to door. Or you could go to Kormann's grocery store and buy ice blocks to pull home in your own little wagon.

Then there was Sam the junk man. The neighborhood was quite clean because we kids used to sell him bottles, cans, aluminum utensils and scrap iron. We would put rocks in the aluminum objects to up the weight—and our payment—and stomp on it to hide it. But Sam got wise to that trick.

Another street vendor was Angelo Baglio. He drove a modern fruits and vegetable truck. His wife, Josephine, was real nice. She bought magazines from me—*Liberty* and *Life*. I would baby-sit for her kids—and I got a nickel.

The Baglios lived next door to "Jackie Johnson." We used

13

to call him that and he would chase us all over the street. His real name was Jim Falbo. His grandson Jimmy Falbo was a good friend of mine.

The Italian families were real close, just as we had been in Swede Hollow. I chummed with Angelo and Louis De Vito, both really great guys from a well-respected family. Louie had a way with the girls. He was nice-looking and had a real line. Angelo was more of the outdoors, strong type.

Louis became a colonel in the U.S. Army and I think Angelo was a master sergeant. Their younger brother Tony hung around with the wrong element and supposedly was snitching to the police about his comrades. He disappeared about 1954, and we all figured he had been murdered. His body was supposedly in Tanners Lake or in the concrete under Interstate 94. But it was never found.

Another young man, who shall remain nameless, was a bright, happy-go-lucky guy. He took a shortcut to fame, first as a pimp for prostitutes and then with a gangster element in Chicago. He was found dead in the trunk of an automobile in the early 1950s, riddled with more than fifty bullets. It's a shame—had he chosen a legitimate profession, I believe he could have gone far in life.

A little earlier, in the 1940s, the crime news hit closer to home when one of the neighborhood residents was found guilty of sex abuse—with his daughters. He was sent off to "college" in Stillwater. College is what we called the Minnesota state prison.

CHAPTER 6

Sunday Sweets

O<small>N</small> S<small>UNDAYS</small> I <small>USED TO GO TO</small> M<small>ASS</small> at Saint Ambrose Catholic Church on lower Payne Avenue. Father Louis Pioletti, from Turin, Italy, was a no-nonsense priest who was loved and respected by the parishioners and feared by the children.

I was usually restless during Mass. My mama and papa would be in the congregation somewhere, but I sat in the kids' section, which was the first three or four rows. When I got too disruptive, Father Pioletti would leave the altar, come to my pew and take me by the ear up to the foot of the altar, where he would sit me down. I wouldn't be alone; there were others who misbehaved who would join me.

When we got older and could sit anywhere in church, on many occasions we would sneak out of church and go downtown to Nardini's Malt Shop and have an ice cream cone. Then we would rush back to church just before Mass was over.

After spaghetti for Sunday lunch at home we would walk to Cardelli's sweet shop, about a mile away, and watch Ed McCormick as he would paste up the major league baseball scores that had come in by ticker tape. This was the highlight of the day for us kids.

Little Italy was slightly more than a mile from the Payne Avenue business district as well as downtown Saint Paul. I was about eight years old when I walked out of the F.W. Woolworth store at Payne Avenue and Case Street with 11 pencils without paying for them.

Several days later my dad caught me with them. He knew

I didn't have the money to pay for them so he started grilling me. I finally confessed that I had stolen them. He gave me the worst whipping I ever had in my life. He accompanied me to Woolworth's to return the pencils. The whipping was worse than the embarrassment. But it did the trick—I never stole anything more in my life.

CHAPTER 7

Dangerous Fun—and Danger

THE STREETCAR RAN IN FRONT OF MY HOUSE on Collins Street. Many times we would pull the emergency cord at the rear of the car to make it stop. The streetcar motorman would be very angry—but by the time he got to the back of the car we would be long gone. On other occasions we would "flip a streetcar"—hang on to a handle in the back of the street car for a ride—sometimes all the way downtown—unnoticed by the conductor or the riders. I think the drivers in the cars following us thought we were crazy—it was dangerous.

I was hit by automobiles twice on Collins Street. I have no recollection of one of the incidents, but in the other, traffic stopped after a car hit me and I fell. But I didn't stay put. I started crawling up the street under the cars. I was found about the fourth car back from the one that hit me. Why I crawled away, I'll never know.

One of my friends, Dominic "Bunky" Caliguire, was a very brave and mischievous kid. Just to show off, he would walk along the railings on the Lafayette Bridge, which were about 4 feet above the bridge roadway and 20 feet above the railroad tracks. He was the only one I knew who did such a foolish and dangerous thing, and he never fell off.

One of the worst sights I saw in my life was at the Lafayette Bridge, where a kid died while flipping a freight. Riding on a train illegally was much more dangerous than flipping a streetcar. We usually hung on the side of a freight car or between two cars.

We often picked up the freight at Lafayette Bridge and jumped off underneath the Edgerton Street bridge, about a mile away. Beyond that point the freight would pick up speed toward its destination.

Flipping a freight was extremely dangerous, but if you were lucky you would find a freight car with an open door and then travel in style. Yes, like a dummy, I flipped freights but *never* got between the cars!! That's what the kid was doing when he fell and was killed. They put his head in a basket and the rest of him in a blanket. I never forgot. How could you?!

CHAPTER 8

Fist Fight of the Month

Most of us kids had a solid bond with one another. Mike Sirian was always one of the smartest kids in school. There was Don Legato, whose dog bit me, and I had to go to Ancker Hospital for stitches. Joe and Lawrence Venaglia, the next-door neighbors, were good guys, despite being Tuscans. Lawrence and I had a fist fight of the month, usually about some petty differences, and he usually, but not always, won.

We had no money—my parents gave me 5 cents a week, which I spent almost every week on a movie. Little brother Albert, Jimmie Falbo, Joe Russo—usually four or five of us would go to the State Theater and see Rin-Tin-Tin or a Tom Mix Western. Going to the show cost my whole 5-cent allowance, but the nice lady who sold tickets always let Albert in for free with me.

I got to see John Wayne in "Hurricane Express" as a serial that ran before the weekly feature. Another movie was "Dracula." I was so frightened by Bela Lugosi's character that I went to bed that night with a crucifix under my pillow.

I was 9 or 10 when my older brother Nick went to work as an usher at the President Theater, a movie house. I'd go along with him to work and sweep out the ushers' break room. Then I could see the movies for free. One of my favorites was shown in 1932, "The Whole Town's Talking," with one of my favorite movie stars, Jean Arthur, and Edward G. Robinson.

Later on, when we kids began to sell newspapers downtown and had a little money, we'd go after the show to the Chicken Shack, a greasy spoon in a very small building on Sibley Street at the corner of East Seventh. We could all afford to buy a hot dog, and if we were flush we would get a pork-chop sandwich. Even with selling papers, I would have to budget my pennies to buy one.

CHAPTER 9

A Newsie from Little Italy

I WAS ABOUT NINE YEARS OLD when I began selling newspapers, or "sheets," on street corners in downtown Saint Paul. I showed early signs of entrepreneurship. I'd establish a location, then turn it over to a kid for a fee. I did this with Dan and Matt Pilla and my brother Albert. I got 5 cents a night from each of them.

I had my own corner at Fourth and Jackson Streets, next to the Great Northern Building. Izzy and Benny Johnson had the newsstand inside the building. Oh, how I envied them! The building was cool in the summer and warm in the winter. I was outside, freezing in the winter and sweating in the summer.

On a good day I would make 40 or 50 cents. Guess what Albert and I did with the money we earned? Most of it, that is. We gave it to our mother.

Being a newsboy opened up a big new world for me. All of my friends had been of Italian descent; now that I was "hustling sheets," I was getting to know kids of different ethnic backgrounds, especially Jewish kids. And I got to meet people from all walks of life.

One nattily dressed gentleman bought a paper from me each night. He would give me a nickel for a 2-cent paper. Boy, was I happy when I saw him coming down the street every day. Forty years later I met him—Benny Price, then the owner of Coleman's Nightclub on Ford Parkway.

A guy I saw only once was looking for a sporting house one afternoon. He gave me a quarter, and I sent him a block and a half up the street on Jackson to the Novotney Sporting Goods

Store. He came back 10 minutes later and said, "Hey, kid, that's not what I had in mind." This time I sent him to the Windsor Hotel, and he didn't come back.

One Christmas a guy approached me and told me he would give me a dollar if I would deliver a package for him to his estranged family. Wow, a dollar! It would take me almost a week to earn that much. Of course I was delighted to do so. He gave me the package, the dollar, streetcar fare and instructions to go to a mini-market at the corner of East Minnehaha and Ruth Streets. If I remember correctly, I left the package at the store for his wife. It must have gone OK as I never saw or heard from him again. It never occurred to me that this delivery was anything but a Christmas gift and not some illegal contraband. The mini-market is still there, one of the few mom-and-pop grocery stores remaining from that era. I drive by it several times a week, and it always brings back memories of that Christmas many years ago.

Newsboys always liked bad news because newspapers would print an extra, the most recent edition with a new front page. Extras sold really well and meant extra cash for the newsie. The extra edition of the Charles Lindbergh son's kidnapping in 1932 was my biggest seller, closely followed by the plane crash of Will Rogers and Wiley Post in 1935. Sometimes the newspaper would overemphasize an event and the edition was a dud. You can fool some of the people some of the time. But not all the time.

On Saturday nights I sold newspapers up and down Saint Peter Street. At the time we had the *Saint Paul Dispatch, Pioneer Press* and *Daily News,* and the *Minneapolis Star, Tribune* and *Journal.* I sold them all, but favored the *Daily News.*

I was in and out of taverns all night. It was 1933. The street was loaded with gangsters, pimps and whores. The G&M and Miller's were the most popular spots on the street. One compensation for hanging out with undesirables—the tips were very good.

The people we worked for were a bunch of characters. Mogey Bernstein was in charge of newsboys at the *Saint Paul Daily*

News. Louis Minuk and Riggi somebody—I never did know his last name—were in charge for the *Saint Paul Dispatch* and *Pioneer Press.* They were all different, strange, what have you. I remember Louie Minuk because he was going with a much younger woman. We all called her "the strawberry blonde." In my opinion, she took him to the cleaners.

One of the highlights of the year was the newsboys' Christmas party at Carling's Cafeteria on Robert Street. Most of us got to eat food there that we had never eaten before, like turkey and dressing, ham, cake.

I was happy when the Jewish holidays came around and I would substitute for a guy called Mace, who took the religious days off.

His paper business was a little different than that of most of us who worked the downtown area, just as he was a little different.

Mace was a little childish. He was about 40, but had the mind of a 12-year-old. Because of his diminished abilities, people went out of their way to help him and he had a lot of special customers among the merchants downtown. So his business was about three times the size of mine. It was profitable to sub for him, even if I did have to hire a sub for my own regular stops—Fourth and Jackson, Seventh and Cedar and the rest.

The downtown assignments were made on the basis of seniority. If you stayed around long enough, you could pick up brisk business when corners opened up as the older newsboys quit. That's how I built up my route from the time I started at the age of nine.

At 14, I retired from selling newspapers.

CHAPTER 10

I Discover Music— and Also That I Am Poor

T<small>HE</small> C<small>HRIST</small> C<small>HILD</small> C<small>OMMUNITY</small> C<small>ENTER</small> on Payne Avenue was our hub of activity, especially in the wintertime. There were basketball games, music lessons, dances and general fooling around.

In 1932, when I was 10, I took guitar lessons at the Christ Child Center from Don Anderson, probably the finest guitarist in the Twin Cities and just a great fellow. The lessons were among the activities sponsored at the center by the Optimists Club. One day a newspaper photographer came, and the next day I saw Anderson's picture in the paper teaching me how to play the guitar. The caption stated that I was underprivileged.

I quit the lessons. I was really offended. I did not feel underprivileged at all.

One night in 1938 I was in the stands watching a basketball game in the gym when a staff member came to the gym overlook and said we were being invaded from Mars. One of the staff people had been listening to the radio in the office and heard about it.

Everybody was frightened to no end. The staff turned up the radio, and except for the excited voices of the news announcers, it was quiet. Everybody was listening.

Then the radio announcer said it was not a true happening, only a radio program. It was Orson Welles with "The War of the Worlds." He had turned H. G. Wells' science-fiction book into a script that was broadcast all the way through without commercials, and it made him famous.

I'd say most of us were all shook up. Many listeners throughout the nation were more than shook up. We thought some people committed suicide, but later that was found to be not true.

CHAPTER 11

"Not Dumb, Just Mischievous"

THE COLLINS STREET HOUSE was right across the street from Lincoln School—very convenient, especially in the cold and snow.

Any time you thought of Lincoln School you couldn't help thinking of Miss Thuet. She was the principal and she was a holy terror. If you ended up in her office because you had been noisy or disruptive, you'd never forget it. She was tough, she'd yell at you, she'd tell you to put your hand out before you. And you knew what was coming—every kid in the school knew it. She'd whack you over the hands with a ruler and, man, you'd feel it.

One time I got a piece of pencil lead embedded in my head, but it wasn't on purpose. A teacher had accidentally hit me on the head and the pencil point broke off. I had to go to the nurse's office to have it removed.

But when Miss Thuet hit you, it was generally on purpose. One time I had been so naughty that she whacked me over the hands, and then put me back a grade.

I had failed an earlier grade at Lincoln. Not because of bad grades. It's true I wasn't an A student but I had good ideas. I thought it would be wonderful if you could hook up wires to a blanket and have electricity keep you warm in bed. And I thought it would be great if automobiles would have windshield wipers on the back windows as well as the front. Both of those ideas came to pass.

No, it wasn't bad grades that made me fail that earlier grade, but bad behavior. This time my mom and brother Nick went to see her on my behalf. Miss Thuet said, "He's not dumb, just mischievous." A week later, she returned me to my proper grade.

If Miss Thuet had punished me in today's world as she did then, I think she would have been fired from her job. I didn't like getting hit, but I think she helped keep me pretty much on the straight and narrow.

CHAPTER 12

Sports, Where I Did Not Excel . . .

A<small>FTER</small> L<small>INCOLN</small>, I <small>WENT TO</small> Cleveland Junior High School. Cleveland went by pretty fast, except for the walking. There were no school buses. Rain or shine, cold or warm, we walked two miles plus each way to school each day.

I was a pretty short kid. Back at Lincoln, we had to line up against the wall for roll call in gym class, the tallest kid first and the shortest last. Just about every year, I alternated being last in line with James Bellamo, who grew up to be a doctor who made house calls well after no one else did.

Being short was a handicap in a lot of sports, but not in boxing. I remember one fight at Cleveland with Mike Morelli. He was about 5-foot-2, and I'm 5-foot-7. I thought it would be easy. But he beat the living crap out of me. He was fast and he was tough.

As a kid, I was on a boxing team for the *Saint Paul Daily News*. We usually fought newsboys from the rival *Saint Paul Dispatch*. I had 12 fights—won five, lost seven. One fight I probably won because my opponent looked worse than I did—really beat up, bloody face and all. But I really should have lost—I was in worse shape but it didn't show. I had a headache for days and my teeth were loose for weeks.

Most of the kids I knew excelled at sports. I did not. I played basketball for a team at the Christ Child Center with Morris Ferrozzo, Paul Pilla, Benny Volpe, Emil Gatto and Phil Carletto. I was the lousiest player on the team, but I was there when we won the championship in 1937.

The trophy got lost. Forty years later I was giving a speech at the

Merrick Center, successor to the Christ Child Center. The director told me there was a trophy in the attic with my name on it and would I like it. I was tickled pink to get it. It gave me "bragging rights" if anyone doubted my sports ability—I'd show them the trophy. I still have it displayed in my little office in the basement of my home.

We kids loved sledding down Brunson Street. We couldn't afford a sled. No matter—we used corrugated boxes instead and had a lot of fun, even though we weren't the Summit Avenue crowd.

A block over was the Hopkins Street Playground—if you could call it a playground. It was an empty lot where we played softball. The field was level to about third base, where it began to rise. The left fielder and the center fielder were about 30 to 40 feet above the level of the third baseman. It was a lousy place to play ball, although it worked out OK for skating.

One early evening I was playing softball, running the bases. When I turned third base, Joe Skipon tripped me. Everyone thought it was funny but me. I didn't sleep at all that night. The next day my brother Nick took me to Ancker Hospital. I had a broken wrist.

Years later, after World War II, Joe Skipon and I became very good buddies. If I wanted to harbor ill feeling toward everyone who pulled a prank on me, I would have no one to associate with.

CHAPTER 13

...And Music, Where I Did

I ALWAYS LIKED MUSIC. My mother influenced my vocalizing with her singing around home, but it was at the Christ Child Center where I learned the tarantella, an Italian folk dance. It involves kicking a leg up and clapping the hands underneath the leg. It can be danced by yourself, or 40 people all in a circle. By the time I was about 10, I had learned it so well that I often danced it for programs given by the center around the community. Once I danced it on a round table at the Ramsey County Home. I was usually accompanied by an adult, often Miss Eleanor Dowling, a kind, dedicated lady and director of the center, God rest her soul.

Long before I bought my saxophone, I was appearing in amateur shows at local theaters. My older brother Nick took me under his wing and booked me into many shows. He was more responsible than anyone for me attaining a musical career.

I was very fortunate that a couple of times my teachers at Lincoln School excused me from classes to pursue my musical career. Probably Miss Thuet and her ruler didn't know about it.

I appeared one afternoon in a talent contest sponsored by radio station WMIN with Jack O'Farrell's Orchestra at the Zephyr Nightclub on Wabasha Street next door to the Strand Theater. I won first prize singing "When My Dream Boat Comes Home." The prize money was about $5.

I won first prize at the Hollywood Theater in South Saint Paul and third prize at the Lyceum Theater in Saint Paul. I remember singing "The Music Goes 'Round and 'Round" and "I'm Sitting High on a Hilltop."

Just about this time, Ted Lewis, of "Me and My Shadow" fame, was at the Orpheum Theater. His act would be condemned today as racist. He danced with a black man behind him—his "shadow" for the song. There was nothing racist about the song, just the way he presented it.

I was selling newspapers at Seventh and Saint Peter Streets. At one of his intermissions I went back to ask if I could have his autograph. I can remember his response to this day. He said to me: "Get away from me, kid—I want to get that sunshine." I was angry and disappointed.

I was so angry, I went home and broke all six of his phonograph records that I owned. And I've never said a good word about him since.

CHAPTER 14

The Radio Bug Bites
in the Fruit Cellar

O NE OF MY HOBBIES AS A KID was collecting 78 rpm phonograph records. Hart Callendar, owner of a record shop on University Avenue near Snelling Avenue, used to give me records in lieu of money for straightening out the records for sale in his store. My collection grew to more than a thousand records.

I used to pretend I had a radio station. I used my mom's fruit cellar downstairs at home as a studio. I would play 78s on a phonograph and doing a little announcing between numbers. I bought some kind of electrical accessory and hooked my microphone to the radio upstairs. But the connection wasn't compatible and I blew the radio out. It made me very unpopular around the house. Maybe that's why, years later during World War II, my mother sold the records without asking me, for a penny and a half apiece. They went toward the war effort to be melted and repressed. It broke my heart to lose them.

One of my customers when I sold newspapers was Jim Bric, the manager of Kesting Music Store on Sixth Street and Cedar Avenue in downtown Saint Paul. Joe Fercello was my dearest buddy at the time, and we would to go visit his uncle, Al Brown, who had the musical-instrument repair department upstairs. Al Brown's last name was really Fercello, too, but at Ellis Island, the person who processed his immigration papers couldn't spell it so the surname was changed to Brown.

Joe introduced me to baseball. We saw so many Saint Paul

Saints games at Lexington Park. We would sit in the bleachers and I would smoke a Harvester cigar—5 cents. The night would cost me a buck total—streetcar ride, bleacher seats and Harvester cigars.

When we would go to the music store, if we weren't talking with Uncle Al, I would listen to 78s, read the sheet music and browse through the beautiful gold-plated musical instruments in the store.

My favorite record was "Who's Sorry Now," by a saxophonist named Harry Roy. I was influenced by that record to want to play the saxophone—a major mistake in a start to a musical career.

The sax has two registers (octaves), compared with the clarinet, which has two and a half registers. Therefore, if you play clarinet, learning the sax comes automatically. If you play sax, you have to work to learn to play clarinet.

I bought a used silver, not gold, alto saxophone for $1.50 a week, which included lessons. If I remember correctly, the whole deal was $65. I could afford it—I had graduated from newsboy to shoeshine boy.

I worked for a Greek fellow named Jim, a nice, easy-going guy who owned the Tip Top Shoe Shop next to the Orpheum Theater on Seventh Street near Wabasha. Later I worked for Chester Mazza, owner of the Wide Awake Shoe Shop on Saint Peter Street across from the original Coney Island sandwich shop. I loved to go across the street and have a coney. The place was owned by the Arvanitis family. The parents worked hard, long hours—he the bar, she the coney section.

The saxophone lessons started when I was 12 or 13. My first teacher, for whom I had no respect, and he shall remain nameless, was bragging about having sex with several underage students. Today he'd be in jail. I quit him early.

My second sax teacher was Hank Capocasa, a good musician. Whenever I hit a wrong note he'd hit me. Wham!! Across the side of my head. Either I had to quit him or I'd end up in a nuthouse. So I quit him.

I then took lessons from Gordy Meek, who had a band at the

Strand Ballroom above the Strand Theater in downtown Saint Paul. He later became secretary, which was and is the most important position, for the musicians union Local 30-73, a post he held until he died in 1999. He was a well-respected and excellent musician and a well-respected gentleman.

CHAPTER 15

Pranks, A. Football, F.

ONE THING NICE ABOUT Johnson High School, it was a half-mile closer each way. And it was more upbeat than Lincoln or Cleveland.

I used to bring stink bombs to school. I'd lay them on the floor and let some unsuspecting student step on them.

I once brought a small portable radio to school. I bought it from a kid with a real bad reputation. Later, other kids told me it was stolen.

The small radio was a novelty then, not commonplace like today. I hid it in a wastepaper basket. Poor, unsuspecting, Miss Lucille Mellem. She was a real nice teacher—I never should have done this to her. I had the radio tuned to the "Ma Perkins" program. Ma was going on about her usual trials and tribulations, and Miss Mellem couldn't determine where the voices were coming from. Finally the jig was up and I ended up in the office of the principal, Mr. Little. He was no Miss Thuet. He bawled me out and that was it. Miss Thuet would have said, "Put your hands out," and cracked them with a ruler.

My cousin Ralph Pariana, son of my dad's cousin Nicola Pariana, was at school with me. Ralph was a down-to-earth type guy and a big football star at Johnson. He was an all-city half-back. Could he run! He was like a gazelle.

I was in the band, under the direction of Mel Smiley, who was also the football coach. I tried out for Johnson football, but I just didn't have it. I was cut from the squad. Not the A team—but believe it or not, the B squad.

My talents ran in other directions, certainly not athletics. I was also bad in math and English, but good in history and biology. Once in art class I drew a picture of Sammy Kaye, well-known as a band leader at that time. Everyone liked it, including the teacher. I was so proud. I don't know what I did with the picture. I usually save everything.

I was pretty good in journalism, too. Franklin D. Roosevelt was president at the time. He had infantile paralysis, later known as polio, and every January, infantile-paralysis fund-raising dances were held throughout the nation to raise money to fight the disease. I wrote a story about the dances for the school paper, the *Courier.* I got up in front of 40 students and read, "The president's balls were held all over the nation last night." The teacher's face was red, my face was red, and the class was mighty quiet.

My strongest point was music.

CHAPTER 16

The Nightclub Scene in High School

In the Johnson High School band, I sat next to Ann Sissini. She was a pretty Italian girl who played better sax that I did. I had a crush on her but she never gave me the time of day. Her brothers Tony and Bob both were excellent musicians. Tony was an excellent trumpet player—he could make that horn sing; Bob was a keyboard artist, and told the lousiest jokes.

Playing in the band at football games at Central Stadium was fun. We musicians had a special section to ourselves in the stands, and my friends and I enjoyed watching the games together between numbers, but beyond that, the band was admired. Next to the football players, the members of the band seemed to get a certain amount of respect and notoriety.

At Johnson I used to "rat" school about once every two weeks. "Rat" means skip. I went to burlesque shows at the Alvin Theater in downtown Minneapolis. The comics were good; the dancers weren't. The pit bands were small, but good.

I'd go to the Orpheum Theater in Minneapolis to see the big bands such as Woody Herman and Jimmy Dorsey. I still have a dollar bill autographed by big-band leader Horace Heidt—a well-known lyricist who wrote the words for "I Don't Want to Set the World on Fire" and "Once in a While"—for participating in his show. He asked for a volunteer. I went up on the stage and sang a song with him.

Even though I was still in high school, I started playing in nightclubs. I was a fairly good musician, a good vocalist and an excellent front man.

My first such job, when I was 15, was at a liquor spot on Dodd Road in West Saint Paul on weekends. Joe Serpico, an accordian player, had organized the trio, which included me on sax and a drummer, whom I don't remember.

The lady who owned the place had just broken up with her boyfriend and every 15 minutes or so she would ask us to play "My Man." The lyrics started, "Oh, my man I love him so, he'll never know," etc. It was a big hit at the time by Ruth Etting, the Peggy Lee of her day.

I played with a variety of musicians in nightclubs such as the Lakeside, Helen's, Traeger's and the Boulevard. My mainstay eventually was Bill Gentile's Bar, where I fronted the Vic Tedesco Trio, with me on sax, Paul Tischler on piano and his brother Eddie on drums. Gentile's bar is now known as the Minnesota Music Cafe. We played at the Wildwood Amusement Park at White Bear Lake before it closed in the late 1930s.

I and quite a few others from the Johnson High School band also played with the 3M Marching Band. We played maybe half a dozen events a year, like the Saint Paul Winter Carnival and neighborhood community events like the Payne Avenue Harvest Festival parade.

My high school pals and I also played for the two bands run by Jolly Stan Federowski. He played concertina when he led the polka band. If we were appearing as the dance band, we changed our "orchestra fronts," the cardboard pieces that fronted our music stands, to say "Lou Barron's Orchestra."

Stan, quite the entrepreneur, had named his dance band to imitate the name of a very popular band at the time, Blue Barron's Orchestra.

We traveled as far as 75 miles to play dates. One winter day on our way to Bay City, Wis., we had to go over the old spiral bridge in Hastings, Minn. We almost slipped off. We were one big bunch of frightened teenage musicians.

For Valentine's Day 1941, about eight of us piled into Stan's

1938 Hudson Airflow to drive in a blizzard to Schafer, Minn. We hauled our instruments behind the car in a trailer. The snow kept people away; there were only four paid admissions that night. Stan usually paid us a dollar or two per job, but that night, we were being paid on commission. My take for the evening was 15 cents.

I and two buddies bought a 1928 Graham in our senior year. It was a four-door sedan, and Hank Landucci, Joe Venaglia and I each pitched in $10 to buy it for $30 from a guy who was so mean he would just as soon punch you as look at you. On the second day we owned it, we were driving around in the Lake Phalen area when we spotted an auto wheel rolling down the hill. Where the heck did that come from? Suddenly the car started going bumpity-bump, bumpity-bump, and we knew we were in trouble. We had to junk the car; the mean guy who sold it to us wouldn't have given us our money back.

I graduated from Johnson High School in May 1941. I was 19—oldest in the class, thanks to my antics in grade school. My younger sister, Mary, had graduated in January 1941, and we got our diplomas at the same time in May.

School days over, I started looking at my options.

PART TWO

The Stateside War

— CHAPTER 17 —

Shoveling Hamburger for a Living

COLLEGE? NO!! I CAN'T RECALL one graduate from my class going to college from Little Italy. None of us could afford it. I certainly didn't give it a thought. We had no grant or subsidy programs such as there are today.

I looked for work for at least two months. I finally found my way to Swift's Packing House. I was at their employment office every morning at 5:30 for a week. The guy in charge of hiring said, "Kid, you must want a job bad enough to be here every morning so early."

I got the job—shoveling hamburger, yes, shoveling coarsely ground hamburger off a clean floor into a big machine that ground it more finely. It was heavy work. The foreman saw that I was having a hard time so he transferred me to pushing carts of Prem cans to the canning department. I alternated with Harold Liefschultz, who in later years became a successful and wealthy real estate agent. It took two of us to keep the packers supplied with cans.

Prem was Swift's canned-meat product that competed with Armour's Spam. Handling the Prem cans was easy, especially after my first job at Swift's, even though it was fast-paced work.

I was fairly happy, even though I was working at a job I didn't particularly like. I played gigs with my band, including the 1942 spring prom for Saint Agnes High School. We played a lot of romantic smoothies like "My Silent Love" that night.

Years later, when I was on the Saint Paul City Council, a woman called to tell me she had a picture of my band at the

I led a big band playing romantic smoothies for the St. Agnes High School
prom in the spring of 1942.

Saint Agnes 1942 prom, and would I like a copy? Is the pope
Catholic?

I was dating my childhood sweetheart, Alvira Corbo. She
lived in my neighborhood, she was of Italian descent as I was,
and also Roman Catholic. I thought we would marry, but big
events were about to change my life.

One day in early December I came out of the Garrick Theater
in Saint Paul and heard a newsboy shouting, "Pearl Harbor
bombed by Japanese." I say to myself, "Where is Pearl Harbor?"
I didn't realize the significance of the news: The United States
was about to enter World War II.

As the war effort got under way, many celebrities came to
town on war bond tours. If the 3M band played, and it often
did, I was there with my saxophone and got to meet actor Pat
O'Brien, actress Carole Landis and many other stars. On one

Just before my brothers and I got into military uniform, the family posed for a portrait in 1942. Seated are my parents, Antonio and Aïda. Standing from left are Albert, Mary, myself and big brother Nick. Nick was the only sibling born in Italy, where he was christened Nicola.

occasion at the Union Depot in Saint Paul, Joe Fercello and I had the opportunity to meet and have our picture taken with Bing Crosby.

Early in 1942 I tried to enlist in the Coast Guard, but I was rejected because I was color-blind. However, that didn't stop the Army from drafting me. I gave Alvira a couple of kisses and said goodbye, assuming she would be there when I came back.

CHAPTER 18

The Beat Goes On, for a Bit

I ENTERED THE SERVICE ON Nov. 4, 1942, at Fort Snelling. I was "shipped out" to Fort Benning, Ga., on a dirty troop train, sleeping in a dirty coach car with 50 to 60 other guys. For the first time in my life I was more than 75 miles from home.

Three days later, we arrived at Fort Benning. Three of my schoolmates from Saint Paul had been on the train, too—Mike Sylvester, Jimmy Maggi and Gene Peterfeso. But we didn't see each other very much once we were at Benning, which was the largest military camp in Georgia. It was basically an infantry camp, but other large units such as the 10th Armored Division were based there, as were the Rangers, supposedly the toughest soldiers in the Army.

Upon arriving, I was interviewed and immediately assigned to the 10th Armored Division Band. I was jubilant.

Our daily routine was great. Breakfast was at 7 A.M.—no kitchen police or guard duty for the musicians. We practiced Army band music in the morning, took an hour off for lunch and practiced dance-band music in the afternoon, playing such tunes as "In the Mood," "One O'Clock Jump" and "Sing, Sing, Sing."

My joy at my musical assignment was short-lived. My first day in the band, one of the musicians was replaced by a member from the Benny Goodman band. I knew my playing days were numbered as one by one the existing members were replaced by musicians from the Glenn Miller, Tommy Dorsey, Artie Shaw and other name bands. I learned a lot of the facts of life from these "big city," big-time musicians. They traveled in much different circles than I did. After getting to know them, I actually appreciated my life style more!

I, too, was soon replaced, by a member of Claude Thornhill's band. I was reassigned to the 3rd Armored Regiment, Company D of the 10th Armored Division. I was so disappointed that I had to leave the band. More than disappointed, I was angry. Because of my attitude, I wasn't a good soldier, not like the guy named Fry, who was exceptionally bright. He always led the entire company in any kind of test we took.

I was assigned menial duties. Guard duty, cleanup crew, KP (kitchen patrol) on Thanksgiving, Christmas and New Year's. I must have peeled hundreds of potatoes. The head chef was a master sergeant nicknamed Frenchy. He was mean and really bossed you around.

Just after New Year's a second lieutenant called me aside and gave me a good talking to. He said that I should straighten out and my Army life would be a lot easier. I did and it did. Within two months I became a corporal—nothing to brag about but "light-years" better than being a private. No more KP or cleanup gangs, and being a corporal of the guard was a lot better duty than guard duty—I got to be in charge of at least two dozen privates pulling 24-hour guard duty. They would be on duty for two hours and then off for four hours.

The corporal of the guard was on duty for eight hours, seeing that the shifts were fulfilled. He had to be around, but not focused constantly. I could read or talk to off-shift guards—light duty.

CHAPTER 19

Competition for the Ladies

But I did not like Fort Benning, probably because the Army was a new way of life. Some of the guys were crude, loud and boisterous. They weren't exactly dirty, but they weren't the epitome of cleanliness either.

Columbus, Ga., was our weekend liberty town, and it wasn't much, either. I did not frequent the night spots or whorehouses— even if I had wanted to, I couldn't. I didn't have any money. I just walked the streets, and at sundown I'd take the bus back to camp. It wasn't prudent for an Army man to be in Columbus, Ga., or Phenix City, Ala., at night. Many soldiers were mugged, beaten up, even murdered. It would have been a waste of a mugger's time to rob me. I never had more than $2 or $3 on me.

My unhappy stay at Fort Benning lasted six months—then came my "best break." I was sent to the armored school at Fort Knox, Ky. I was overjoyed to say the least. The accommodations were the same as Fort Benning—an Army camp is an Army camp. But the routine was different. I had no extra duties of any kind. I wasn't even issued a rifle. Being a student was much nicer than being a soldier.

During the week I was learning electrical circuitry in the M1 tanks. On weekends I was going to Louisville, Ky., instead of Columbus, Ga. I went to the USO (United Service Organization) and the YMCA (Young Men's Christian Association) and the YMHA (Young Men's Hebrew Association) and met a lot of nice people.

Competition for the ladies was rough in the towns near Army

bases. In Columbus, the ratio of men to women must have been 40 to 1, and I never had a date in Georgia. Even in Louisville it had to be 20 soldiers to every woman. At Fort Knox itself, our barracks were next to a battalion of the Women's Army Corps (WACs). But they weren't interested in us enlisted men, they went after the officers.

I remember I liked a WAC from Oil City, Pa. But I couldn't even get her to go to the post theater with me.

I met a very nice woman at the Louisville USO, whose name I've forgotten. After all, it was 60 years ago. She was older than me, a schoolteacher who lived in a nice house by herself. She invited me over several times. To be in a comfortable home is so much nicer than being in an Army barracks with dozens of soldiers around. But we were different. We just didn't hit it off, so I went on my way.

CHAPTER 20

Finding Home Away from Home

O<small>NE NIGHT</small> I <small>WAS WALKING</small> down the street in Louisville and I see a sign: "De Camilli's Bar." I knew it had to be Italian, so in I went. It was owned by an Italian couple from Cumberland, Wis. I learned there were a lot of Italian families in Louisville. Soon I was invited to Italian homes for dinner. Finally, I had a social life on weekends to offset my dreary daily Army routine.

The De Camillis introduced me to Esther Currella. I really liked her. I took her to see the movie "Stage Door Canteen," my first real date in the Army. The romantic "spark" wasn't there, but we became real good friends—went to social gatherings, Italian parties.

I went to another Italian bar, Gargotto's—and met a very pretty and nice lady whose maiden name had been Dolly Capra. She was from a very respectable family who lived three blocks away from me in Little Italy when we were growing up, but now she was married to Al Colyard, another guy from our old neighborhood. He was in the Merchant Marines based in Louisville, and she had followed him there.

I loved hanging out at Gargotto's. Every Saturday night I danced with Dolly, who didn't have a hole in her stocking. A version of "Buffalo Gals" was a big song hit at the time—"I danced with a dolly with a hole in her stocking." Another popular tune on the jukebox was "Don't Fence Me In." I never got to see Al—he was so busy he even worked Sundays. But Dolly was sure good to me. It was easy for her, she had a pleasant personality and made you feel wanted and important. She introduced me to many of the locals, mostly women.

I also started hanging around at a shoeshine shop owned by a guy named Earl Eckerle, who invited me to his home several times to have dinner with his family. Earl's shoeshine partner was nice enough, not very friendly, handsome, about 45 years old—too old to be drafted, so he had a parade of women. The ladies really liked him.

I met another important person in my life in Louisville, Ky.—Jimmy Atria, a soldier from New Jersey who was married to the sister of Pee Wee Reese, of Brooklyn Dodgers baseball fame. Jimmy and I were great friends—we were very compatible.

CHAPTER 21

Furlough Time

My weekends were busy in Louisville—De Camilli's and Gargatto's and Earl's and many invitations to private homes for dinner. I had it made. But, alas, it came to an end within a few months. My stint at the Armored School was over and I was ordered to return to the 10th Armored Division.

First I went on furlough. Fort Knox was relatively close to home—it was overnight by train to Saint Paul. Three days with a weekend pass equaled four and a half days, so I was able to spend three days at home—though it didn't seem much like home. My brother Albert was on the USS *Colorado* in the Pacific and Nick was with the Army engineers in the Philippines. Nick and Al kept the family well-informed as to their well-being by sending letters to my parents at least once a month. I sent Ma and Pa a letter at least once a week, but I'm sure that was because I had more time to do so.

Saint Paul had gone wild. There must have been a dozen bars on Wabasha Street between Kellogg Boulevard and Exchange Street—and all of them hoppin'. And the strawberry blonde (now 10 years older) who had been the girlfriend of my paperboy boss was making the bar scene. I don't know what happened to the boss, Louie Minuk. Everyone seemed to be having a good time while the boys were in foxholes all over the world.

I cut my furlough a little short because I wanted to spend a little time in Louisville with my friends. I said good-bye to my mom and pop and sis, and I went back to Kentucky. I intended to head for the base to wait for my transfer back to Fort Benning, but I learned the 10th Armored Division was on maneuvers in

I was able to come home on furlough several times during World War II.
In 1944, I posed with my dad.

Tennessee. No one seemed to know what company was where. I actually spent two days AWOL trying to find my unit. That worked in my favor. I covered my extra time in Louisville without question. When I finally joined my outfit in the field, no one seemed to care I was late. There was utter confusion.

CHAPTER 22

Leaving the Chiggers Behind

The Tennessee maneuvers were my first experience at soldiering, and it wasn't fun. We bathed in dirty streams, ate from mess kits—sometimes in the rain—and slept on the hard ground in pup tents. I took to sleeping on the canvas tops of trucks. The canvas, stretched over slat frames, became sort of like a hammock. It was more comfortable than pup tents, but extremely dangerous—if you fell off, most likely you'd be seriously injured. And the chiggers were everywhere, day and night.

One day when maneuvers were almost over, our company battalion practiced donning gas masks and then wearing them in a gas chamber. When I came out I was extremely uncomfortable. I had difficulty taking off the gas mask—my face had swollen up tremendously. I was rushed to the medical camp, where it was determined I was probably allergic to the rubber material in the mask and I shouldn't wear one.

The 10th was ordered out of Tennessee to Camp Gordon, Ga., instead of Fort Benning. I was sent to the Camp Gordon hospital for allergy tests. Funny how you remember little things, like the Mills Brothers singing "Paper Doll" during my hospital stay.

The medics found I was allergic to pork, citrus acids and certain pollens, among other things. I was put on a special diet. Wow!!

I had kitchen privileges. I was allowed to go into the cooler and pick out what I wanted to eat. I was the envy of the company.

I also got to be company clerk—which was a cushy job. I did my duties—but I had plenty of time on my hands, so I started up my fictitious radio station, like I had when I was a kid in my mom's fruit cellar.

Now I was a grownup and had a typewriter and a real desk, so I used to type up fictitious radio logs. At first my call letters were the old ones, WVIC, from the fruit cellar. Then I pretended that my station was WFKY, Frankfort, Ky. I would list different programs—news, interviews, music, for every half hour, not like today's radio stations, which play the same tunes over and over for 24 hours. Each half-hour program had a title, "Today's Hits," "Memory Time," "Cowboy Corral," and even a classical music concert. I wish I would have kept some of the logs—would have been interesting to compare them with the real ones I wrote later as an owner of radio stations.

Eventually Frankfort got a station called WFKY but I had nothing to do with it. One of the young ladies from the USO, Jane Haga, became a longtime employee of WFKY. She did a host of duties, from secretarial work to copy writing and preparing logs—quite common in a small radio station.

CHAPTER 23

The Latrine Is in Order, Sir!

M**Y STAY AT CAMP GORDON** was short-lived. The Army was streamlining the 10th Armored Division, and in the spring of 1943 three tank battalions were reassigned. The 785th was deployed to the Pacific. I don't know what happened to the 779th, but my 777th Tank Battalion was attached to, of all places, the Armored School at Fort Knox, Ky.

I was so very happy I was going to be back near Louisville—heaven compared to Columbus or Augusta, Ga.

Duty at Fort Knox was bearable. Our permanent barracks at the main post was like a big brick apartment building, rather than the stereotypical wooden barracks we had at Fort Benning. We made a lot of field trips, but they lasted only overnight.

One day the entire camp was to stand for general inspection by Gen. Robinette, commander of the Fort Knox Army post. Our company commander wanted a noncommissioned officer to stand guard over the latrine—yes, the latrine. No one wanted the duty—it wasn't dignified. Cpl. Tedesco took it.

When the general entered the barracks, I had to tell him the latrine was in order, sir. This was at 9 A.M. After the general left, I left the camp and made it to Louisville before noon. After all, my job was over. I learned later that the entire camp was under inspection until 6:30 P.M.

I was still corresponding with my sweetheart back home, Alvira Corbo. She and I had been not too happy about my having to leave for the Army, but she said she would write to me often, which she did. She also said she'd wait, which she didn't.

At Fort Knox I got a "Dear Vic" letter from her. She was going to marry Emil Truskolowski. I called her from a phone near my barracks. Told her I'd get an emergency furlough and come home and we'd marry. But she said no. I think it was a case of his being there and my being elsewhere. I was heartbroken, but we remained friends until her death nearly 60 years later.

CHAPTER 24

I Find the Swingin' Town

At least once a week the company would hear rumors that we were being shipped overseas. That irritated me—so I started a rumor that the 777th Tank Battalion was being shipped overseas in two days. Lo and behold, within six hours the whole building was abuzz that we were going overseas in two days. Well, it didn't happen.

But something of great importance did happen. The 777th Tank Battalion was attached to the 69th Infantry Division to be shipped out to England. They would be practicing for the invasion of occupied Europe. Me, with my allergy to gas masks, I was transferred out. Guess I was a lucky so-and-so.

I was assigned to be an instructor at the Armored School— electrical circuits in the M1 tank. Instead of being the student, I was now the teacher.

At the school, I had a new class of officers and enlisted men every two weeks. One of my students was a Captain Tedesco. The students referred to us as the captain and the corporal.

I had two years of service in with nothing bad on my record, so I was promoted to buck sergeant. I was a good, not great, soldier.

But buck sergeant was good enough to make me a tank commander on short training maneuvers in rural Kentucky. They were live-ammo maneuvers, and one of the soldiers in my tank was seconds away from having his head blown off because he stuck his head outside of our tank in front of a machine gun. Lucky for him and for me, he ducked back inside just in time.

I'm sure I would have faced disciplinary action, possibly dishonorable discharge, had he been killed while I was in charge.

One of my circuitry students, a Pvt. Franco from Red Bank, N.J., asked me where I was going for the weekend. I told him, Louisville, of course. He said, why go to Louisville where there are 20 soldiers for every girl? Grab a bus or hitchhike up to the capital, Frankfort, where there are four girls for every soldier. I took his advice, and he was right.

Frankfort, like Saint Paul, was a swingin' town. It seems like every town of any size was really hopping during the war.

When I first got to Frankfort, I made the bar scene. There were girls everywhere and not too many men around. I don't remember any young lady refusing to dance with me. It was the 1940s, I was a single Army guy, so I did what most single Army guys did: I usually went home with a different young lady each weekend and stayed at her apartment.

One lied to me—told me she was single. I was at her house one night, drinking and smooching, when there was a knock at the door. It was her husband, home on leave. I exited out the back door like a streak of lightning. This situation made me think I would get shot and no Purple Heart for valor.

CHAPTER 25

My Brownette and Me

Aғтеʀ I had to leave that apartment without notice, I quit the nightclub scene. It was kind of dangerous anyhow. One night I had been walking down the street when I heard a woman in an alley screaming. A guy was beating her up. I went in to help her—they both started beating up on me. I got out of there in a hell of a hurry.

I now started to hang around the USO. There were 19 young ladies who were volunteers who started the club on the third floor

Young ladies of Frankfort, Ky., made the USO a swell place to hang around.
My brownette, Vickie Calvert, is standing, second from left.
Her friend Mary Haney is standing at left.

of an old building on the main street of downtown Frankfort. It was surrounded by bars and retail stores.

It was a friendly place. Dear old Florence Hargins would play piano and sing "Let the Rest of the World Go By" for the soldiers, most from Fort Knox and a few home on leave. But there weren't too many of us. I remember 22 soldiers at a big Christmas party in 1944.

I was 21, and I started to date pretty young women in their late teens. I was invited to their homes for Christmas, Easter, etc., and I was treated like royalty.

I dated two of the USO young ladies. The first was Jeanne Morrow. We were nice to each other—nothing serious, only three or four dates. Then I fell head over heels for a pretty brownette, Victoria Calvert. She had a real nice girl friend, Mary Haney, a little on the plump side. I had a friend at camp, Herb Freundt, a little on the plump side. You guessed it—I fixed them up. They married during the war.

Herb, Mary, Victoria and I double-dated quite often. One night

Vickie Calvert and I went together for 22 months. After we broke up, I didn't go steady with anyone for the rest of my Army days.

at the American Legion Club in Frankfort we ran into a guy the locals called "Captain Hook." He was a mean troublemaker with a metal hand. He wanted to fight with me—and me, a dummy with a little too much booze in me, wanted to go outside with him. He would have killed me, and that's what happened to him—the following week someone shot him to death.

Another day I was with Vickie at her sister Imogene Riddle's house and we were goofing around. Vickie painted my fingernails with clear polish. I stayed overnight at the USO and the next afternoon I was having lunch when I met up with an acquaintance I was pretty sure was gay. His actions were very feminine. When he saw my hands with the fingernail polish, he must have thought I was gay, too. He wanted me to go for a ride in his car. I told him to forget it. He backed off quickly when he realized he had made a mistake. I didn't let Vickie paint my nails again.

I went with Vickie for 22 months. I named a tank after her: "Calvert's Pride." I bought a miniature toy tank for her and had her name painted on its side. Everyone thought we would marry—so did I.

But her parents didn't like me. I was a Yankee, an Italian and a Catholic. It didn't bother Vickie, but I knew it bothered them. In any event, we broke up and I didn't go steady with any ladies the rest of my Army life. I really had cared for her.

CHAPTER 26

I Land in the Brig in Saint Paul

I KEPT UP WITH NEWS FROM HOME through letters from the folks but also with a newsletter sent to Saint Paul men in service by the Christ Child Community Center, where I had spent so much time in my youth. The newsletters were put together by Gentile "Gindy" Yarusso, who was then a sort of social worker there.

But I got my news firsthand, too, because the trip from Fort Knox to Saint Paul was relatively easy. I was able to go home on furlough about every six months.

First I would catch a bus or hitchhike from camp to Louisville. Once it was on a motorcycle. Thirty-two miles on a bike was not very pleasant. It was my first and only ride on a bike.

In Louisville I would catch a train to Chicago, where I had to spend the night. That was a usually a drag—I had no money for a hotel room. I usually stayed overnight sleeping at the Woods Theater, which showed second-run movies for 24 hours. I don't remember any of them. I went to sleep and I'm sure I wasn't the only one. It was a good-size theater, but usually less than half-full.

It was a second-rate movie house, but all I could afford. On one of my trips I did splurge. I went to the Bandbox, a popular night spot in a basement in downtown Chicago, to listen to Boyd Raeburn's Big Band, a powerhouse of a band in the Stan Kenton style.

I would catch an early train the next morning. After the Woods, the coach to Saint Paul was a luxury. I usually slept all the way home, where I would arrive in the afternoon.

On my first few trips, everyone was so happy to see me, but as I came home the third and fourth time, the welcome wore off. One guy, Barney, a neighbor who lived on North Street, wanted to know why I wasn't overseas. He was much older than me, but of draft age. I answered, "Why aren't you in the Army?" That shut him up.

Still, I had some terrific furloughs. Saint Paul was a swinging town. I was with my dear friend and fellow musician Earl Lord one night in downtown Saint Paul at the G&M Bar, not one of your fancy clubs. This one gal was telling me how much she cared for me—and me, like a dummy, I believed her. Well, I had to leave to catch a train for Chicago. I kissed her good-bye—kind of liked her. Got a letter from Earl several days later. Not to worry, he said. She went home that night with another soldier.

One time I was caught home before my furlough started when MPs at the Union Depot asked to see my papers. I usually used a phoney 36-hour weekend pass that started at noon Saturday—but I'd be home Saturday night, which was impossible. I'd never gotten caught before, but I spent the night in the brig at the depot. The next morning I was sent back to camp. I caught hell from my captain. I thought I would lose my sergeant's stripes. But I didn't.

CHAPTER 27

I Lose a Sweetheart to Peace

In the spring of 1945, I met the second lady I really cared for while I was in the Army. The first had been Vickie Calvert. Trudi Roberson I met near her high school in New Albany, Ind., which was across the Ohio River from Louisville.

Trudi was special, a delightful, pretty blonde, a bubbly young lady. I was robbing the cradle—she was 17 and I was 22.

I took her to see a movie, "The Phantom of the Opera" with Claude Raines. Even went to a couple of high school events, and took her to her high school prom. I bought her an orchid corsage—she was so pleased. Our romance could have bloomed, but once again, big events were about to change my life.

V-E Day, May 8, 1945, had ended the fighting in Europe, but Japan was still on the attack in the Pacific Theater. In August 1945 I was assigned special duty away at Lebanon Junction, Ky., about 30 miles from Fort Knox. I was acting 1st sergeant of a battalion (144 men) of 18-year-old soldiers. They had been drafted at 18 but couldn't be sent overseas until they were 19. We were out in the field with pup tents, calisthenics, marching and so on.

Then came V-J Day, August 14, 1945. The war with Japan was over. We were overjoyed. We were miles from civilization, that is, from women and booze, so the men were dancing with each other on the dirt of Mother Earth. We were so happy.

I was assigned to the American military government in South Korea. I had to leave Fort Knox and my friends in Frankfort. It was one of the saddest days of my life. I just hated to leave them.

I didn't see Vickie when I left. We had dated on a couple of occasions after we broke up, but the spark was gone for both of us. I did go to New Albany to say good-bye to Trudi. She was sad to see me go!! She promised to write!!

I gave a soldier friend about a dozen letters addressed to my mom and dad and asked him to mail a letter once a week. I did not want to worry them, and the letters would make them think I was still at Fort Knox and all was well.

I was shipped out to P.O.E. (point of embarkment) Camp Stoneman, Calif., with a group of soldiers from all over the country. I didn't know a single one of them. The night before we were scheduled to ship out for South Korea, broadcaster Walter Winchell comes on the air and says only volunteers will be sent overseas. I was offered a staff sergeant rating if I would volunteer, but I said no, thank you. Only two of the 144 volunteered to go. One of them was from Saint Paul. I saw him two years later—he was a bartender at the Flame Bar. He said I didn't miss a thing and he should have left when I did.

CHAPTER 28

The Beat Is Back

In September 1945, waiting at Camp Stoneman to be discharged to go home, I got another lucky break. I was assigned to special services—the band. This time I got to play and stay, as the star musicians were not coming but leaving. We used to play "Sentimental Journey" for departing troops.

One afternoon I was practicing with the band and a soldier walks in the hall and throws his cap at me. It was Dominic "Bunky" Caliguire, the kid from Little Italy who scaled the railings on the Lafayette Bridge. How happy I was to see him. I was new at camp and didn't know too many people. Bunky and I spent the afternoon together. We went to the PX, and he told me of his prisoner-of-war experiences at the hand of the Nazis in Europe. He was quite a bit underweight—he was given very little food to eat each day. He was real glad to be back in the good old U.S.A.

I spent a lot of my free time in San Francisco. One night I'm in a shady district and I went to a bar called Finocchio's. I left after one drink and was walking down the street when all of a sudden an Oriental guy came running out of an alley toward me yelling, "Help, Joe!" He was all spattered with blood. He was cut up pretty bad—and I wanted no part of it. I took off like a big bird. I remembered the night in Frankfort when I tried to help a lady who was being beaten by her boyfriend and then she and her boyfriend started beating up on me.

On another occasion, I was standing in front of the Palace Theater and a Marine came walking by. He said, "Hey, I know

you—Tedesco." It was Pat Cucchiarella, known as Pucka, looking more handsome in his uniform than he had back home,
driving an ice cream truck in his delivery man's suit.

He was a godsend to me. He took me to a bar outside of the
loop on Van Ness and introduced me around. Everyone knew
him and everyone liked him. He lived in a private residence; he
had special duty right in town as a recruiting officer. He loved
the Marines. In later years, his rec room in his Maplewood home
was loaded with Marine paraphernalia. I think some of my buddies regretted leaving the service—returning to boring jobs in
civilian life.

CHAPTER 29

The Tomato Factory

I DATED THREE YOUNG LADIES while in the Frisco area. One was a young lady with a distinctive last name, Donna Quartamus. Another young lady—I've forgotten her name completely—was a very religious person, Baptist, I think. She talked too much about religion. Later in life I probably would have appreciated her, but just then, I didn't want to get involved. I just wanted to go home!!

The third girl's last name was Rodriguez. She was very nice, and her parents liked me. They were very good to me, invited me to their home.

I met Miss Rodriguez while working at a tomato factory. I heard about the job through some of the soldiers in camp who were working 3 to midnight shifts at the steel mills or tomato factories. I couldn't do this as my day wasn't done until 4:30 P.M., but I got on the good side of the captain so he would change my hours.

The captain was a devout Christian Scientist who had tried to convert me. We hit it off nicely because I listened respectfully. Of course, there was no way I was going to leave my Catholic religion.

I started working in the steel mill, but I found the job too difficult and dangerous. Lifting steel slabs and being so close to the open pit furnaces was not for me. I left to go to the tomato-canning factory, where I fed tomatoes onto a conveyor belt that fed them into a heated vat. The work was easier, and there were some nice women to talk to—much better conditions than at the steel mill. I saved $750 for the four months I worked.

CHAPTER 30

Singing in Solitude All the Way Home

Finally the time came for me to go home in February 1946.

The Army would pay you mileage if you had transportation home. The old brain started working. Next to the USO was a 1928 Reo jacked up on blocks. I bought it from a soldier for $25. He gave me the title card.

I went in to see the Christian Scientist captain and showed him the title card. He looked at me with a grin and said, "Sergeant, do you think you'll make it home in that?" He knew what I was up to, but he OK'd it.

I got $178 to pay for the 2,000-mile trip home. Then next day I sold the Reo for $20.

That night I went down to the railway station, where a troop train was headed for Camp McCoy, Wis. I talked to the mess sergeant and asked him if I could bum a ride home. He told me if I would break 500 eggs a night I could go home with them. I agreed.

Actually, it was good duty. I'd break eggs and sing to myself. I was the only person in the kitchen car all night long. I could eat anything I wanted, so my meals were free. And I got to sleep in a bed instead of a coach seat.

The trip home was beautiful. I got to see a lot of scenery and had a lot of solitude, a relief after the company of soldiers for three and a half years.

I left the train when I got to Omaha, Neb. The mess sergeant gave me a big Velveeta cheese to give to my mom and I bought an $8 coach train ticket to Saint Paul—home.

PART THREE

Radio Days

CHAPTER 31

Getting Back to Music

WHEN I GOT OFF THE TRAIN, I got on the streetcar and headed straight home.

The first person I greeted was my mom. Was she happy to see me, and me her.

The next thing I did was to go to Saint Ambrose Church. It was there I could get to see all my friends, my buddies who had come home from the war and a lot of the old timers who didn't go off to the service.

I settled down at home with my parents. I shared a bedroom with brother Albert. Pretty darn nice after an Army cot. My sister Mary had her own room; Nick was married and no longer living at home.

Then I had to figure out what to do for a living. I was quite frugal, so I was OK financially for a while. I had the $750 I made in the tomato plant and $150 left from my trip money. In 1946 $900 was a lot of money, at least I thought so.

I started selling clothes at Rossman's in downtown Saint Paul. I worked Monday nights, Friday nights and all day Saturday. I looked forward to getting my $20 check every Saturday night at the end of my day's work. The money went to my mom every week for room and board during the two years I lived at home before I got married. I also worked for Angelo Vitali, who used to run with my brother Nick, but I didn't last long.

Angelo was a lot of fun to be with—we called him Six-Gun. He used to like to sing a song called "Outside of You," which I eventually started playing and singing with my small band.

Angelo had a "pop truck" and I would deliver cases of pop off the truck to locations on his route. That wasn't too bad, but he also sold Chippewa Spring water, and we had to lug five-gallon jugs of water around. Some of the locations were brutal—up or down steep flights of steps. I quit about a month later. Today I couldn't lift any of those jugs if my life depended on it.

I led a band at Gentile's Bar Thursday, Friday and Saturday night for $18 plus free drinks from patrons in return for playing their song requests. I was on saxophone and vocals, and acted as MC. Sometimes we had Jim Hobbins on piano, but usually I played with Paul Tischler on piano and Eddie Tischler on drums.

I also played with Bob Sissini, one of my high school bandmates, after the war. With him on keyboards and me on sax, we played at weddings, parties and so on. He now is retired in Hugo, Minn., and plays piano gratis several days a week, performing luncheon concerts at Woodwinds Hospital in Woodbury. On alternate days, the pianist is Phil Kormann, who used to own Kormann's grocery store in Little Italy.

CHAPTER 32

Stage Fright

I STARTED TO ADD COMEDY NUMBERS to my gigs to upgrade my value as a performer in Twin Cities music circles.

I was performing numbers such as "I'm the Greek ambassador, peace on you, my friends" and "I'm the rich maharaja of Magador." As the Greek I put on a long black tuxedo-type coat and a black top hat. The maharaja called for a long-sleeved white silk shirt and a turban. My biggest hit was "Josephina, please no lean-a on the bell." For that I wore a long nightgown and a nightcap with a tassel. I carried a candle in a holder and had a cigar in my mouth—but neither the cigar nor the candle would be lit.

My reputation as an all-around entertainer began to grow, and three different nightclubs offered me work. My big break arrived when I was to appear at Jimmy Hegg's restaurant in downtown Minneapolis in a stage show with Patti Page, an up and coming female vocalist. She was very nice to me, just as she was 50 years later when my band opened for her at the Taste of Minnesota.

I did my "Josephina, please no lean-a on the bell" routine. I got stage fright and forgot some of the words. It was the worst performance of my musical career. The audience was sympathetic, but I was a flop, and I knew my shot at the big time was lost. At the time I was devastated, but in retrospect, I'm glad. I had a wonderful, normal life, something I may or may not have had as a big-time star.

CHAPTER 33

Florence

After that embarrassment, I knew I would not be able to make a living as an entertainer. So I went to school under the GI Bill. I went to a freight-traffic institute to be a dispatcher for a freight trucking company. I knew almost immediately the work didn't appeal to me and I wasn't going to do something for the rest of my life that didn't appeal to me. At least I did learn to type.

In July 1946 I was still playing nights at Bill Gentile's bar. One night the prettiest young lady I ever saw walks into the place. When I saw her I said, "That's for me."

I moved in quickly. I went to the booth where she was sitting with a girl friend. I wanted to buy them a drink, but she said she didn't drink so I got them Cokes.

I telephoned her at home—was nice to her mother and sisters. She and her girlfriend came back to Gentile's. I started dating her. We didn't go anywhere special. I didn't have any money to speak of. Fortunately, for my sake, neither did she. In April 1947 we got married in a very nice church wedding at her home parish, Holy Redeemer Catholic Church in downtown Saint Paul. She was beautiful in her white gown and veil.

The wedding reception was at the American Hall on Payne Avenue, formerly known as the Italian Hall. When Italy joined forces with Germany in World War II and fought America, the name had to go.

That night the hall was filled with people enjoying a two-piece band, all I could afford. Florence was coming upstairs to the main hall when four or five guys "stole her away"—whisked her to an automobile and took off. I wasn't too concerned as stealing the bride was the custom in those days. About an hour later, the bride was brought back unharmed and as beautiful as ever.

We didn't have a honeymoon, just went home to our rented one-bedroom apartment in a fourplex at 498 North Street. It cost $18 a month, with utilities additional.

We lived right next to the Orsello family, where Joe the ice man used to live when I was a kid. Joe was long gone, but we had an ice box. To get ice, we would walk our Radio Flyer wagon to Kormann's grocery store, about six blocks away, load up a couple of blocks and trundle home. Fortunately, we didn't have to do that in the winter because the first thing I bought when I could afford it was a new refrigerator—$5 down and a payment book for $5 a month from Bannon's Department Store.

Actually, it was my dad who bought the refrigerator for us. Appliances were in short supply after the war, but he worked for Bannon's and was able to work a deal for us.

We also had a used washing machine that wasn't worth a darn. Within six months of our marriage, we bought a new one and had a second monthly $5 payment going to Bannon's.

Florence worked in an office at 3M, in whose band I had played in high school, while I played in the band three nights a week and went to school during the day. I'd get home before Florence so I did the housework. It was easy—no kids to mess up the house. Afterward I'd walk to 3M and walk Florence home.

We didn't have much—but we were happy. We didn't even own a car. Everything was within walking distance—3M, Gentile's, downtown Saint Paul.

CHAPTER 34

Radio Days

Playing in the band at night was my anchor. I could depend on music. I knew I was going nowhere fast selling clothes part-time, but I couldn't seem to find a daytime job that was satisfying.

I worked at a battery factory for three days just to make the rent. My clothes were ruined by the acid spilling all over them. I didn't think I could afford having to buy new work clothes all the time, so I left.

Then I tried U.S. Bedding Co., where I had to dip iron rails into a vat of paint. Once again, I would have had to spend a fortune on replacing ruined work clothes.

Working at the Saint Paul Co. as a file clerk was much better. It was clean work, and I wore nice shirts, ties and trousers. But when I could not get prorated vacation time after 11 months, I quit.

I had been dreaming about radio for a long time. As a kid I held forth in the fruit cellar; as an Army clerk in Kentucky with not much to do I typed up radio logs.

In 1948, I decided to go to Brown School of Broadcasting, now known as Brown College. My voice was high-pitched, not a good radio-voice quality, but I wanted to learn the ins and outs of everyday radio station routine.

My brother Albert, who had a beautiful voice, had already graduated from the Beck School of Broadcasting. He started at KDHL in Faribault, Minn., as a full-time radio announcer, then went to KATE in Albert Lea to manage their studios in Austin, Minn.

He subscribed to a radio-industry trade magazine called *Broad-casting* and passed the copies to me after he read them.

One ad in the magazine kept gnawing at me. "Let me build your radio station from the idea to the complete station," it said. Finally I called the person named in the ad, Larry Andrews of Davenport, Iowa. I told him I represented a group (which I did not—it was just me) that wanted to build a radio station in Stillwater, Minn. He said to send him $100 and he would come to Saint Paul and we'd talk about it. I said OK.

I talked to my brother Albert and James Hobbins, at the time the piano player in my group at Gentile's. I talked to my brother Nick, but he was cautious and was not interested in the initial overture.

Larry Andrews came to Saint Paul by train and we all met at Florence's and my apartment. He laid out the fees he required: Pay me (1) $750 ($100 already paid) when the application is filed with the Federal Communications Commission (FCC), he said, (2) $750 more when the application is accepted, (3) $750 when application is granted, (4) $750 when building gets started and (5) another $750 when construction is completed.

Al, Jim and I raised the initial $750. In the meantime, Nick joined us. He had money, which helped our financial standing with the FCC.

We made two $750 payments to Andrews before we wised up and hired an attorney, Abe Stein, of Washington, D.C., to help with the licensing process. Personally, I think Andrews just wanted to get the initial $750 out of us. He could see we didn't have much money. Was he honest? We'll never know. We told him to get lost because we felt he bilked us. To the best of my knowledge he stayed in business in Davenport, Iowa.

We finally got a letter from the FCC stating that our application was in order, but a financial letter of support would get us the license. We knew once we got the license, lenders would be knocking our doors down to get our business. So brother Nicholas approached Lou Sansone of Saint Paul Wreckage Co., asking her for a loan of $15,000 to our group. We got the letter, we got the license, and we were in business. Thanks to Lou for a letter we never used and Nick for getting it.

William F. Johns of the Ridder-Johns group, which had ties to the *Saint Paul Dispatch-Pioneer Press,* was the person who loaned us money. Nick put in 22.5 percent with his own money, and Johns put in 77.5 percent of the capital to build the station—22.5 percent for his own share and 22.5 percent each to brother Al and me for our shares, plus a loan of 10 percent to Jim Hobbins, who sold his shares during the early stages of the operation.

We signed on for the first time at 6:15 A.M. on March 1, 1949, from the broadcast studio in Stillwater. The call letters were WSHB. The letters had been assigned by the FCC, but we told everyone it stood for White Bear Lake, Stillwater, Hudson and Bayport.

The program day, which ran from sunup to sundown, was a typical station format from the 1940s—15 minutes of news, different types of music, local topics, religious programs, kids' shows. It was a real mishmash of this and that.

Johns was general manager, Nick was sales manager, Al did the announcing and I was music librarian, picking all the music played. I also was a part-time radio-ad salesman, and "Uncle Vic."

"Uncle Vic's" 5 P.M. show was the most popular on the air. I read kids' stories and played kids' recorded stories such as "Cinderella" and "Jack and the Beanstalk." One summer day "Uncle Vic" had a picnic at Lowell Park that attracted more than 700 kids. And when I walked up and down the streets of Stillwater, dozens of young people would follow me as if I were the Pied Piper of Hamlin.

The show continued for 15 to 20 years. Years after I was host, one of my successors was Rog Erickson, who later joined with Charlie Boone for "The Boone and Erickson Show" on WCCO radio.

CHAPTER 35

The Split for South Saint Paul

ALL WAS ROSY AT THE STATION for a while. Then William F. started getting less serious about the radio business when he became smitten with his secretary. Tension started to grow in the office with him taking long lunches and afternoons off at the beach. Eventually he divorced his wife and married the secretary.

To us, Johns said: "Buy me out, or I'll buy you out."

The group had invested $18,000. Nick had money but Al and I did not. We sold out to Johns for $87,000.

We had an alternate plan. Johns wanted a covenant that would prohibit us from building a radio station within 50 miles of Stillwater. We said OK, but we put in a clause excluding the Twin Cities. We filed for a station in South Saint Paul, maybe 30 miles away.

Johns was madder than hell. If he had gone to court, he might have made the case that South Saint Paul is part of the Twin Cities and prevented us from building there. But time proved that it didn't matter, as there wasn't any competition whatsoever for advertising clients.

CHAPTER 36

From Cow Kickin' to City Rockin'

SOUTH SAINT PAUL WAS A SMALL TOWN in the shadow of the two big towns, Minneapolis and Saint Paul. We called the station WCOW in honor of the town's main industry, the livestock shipping yards. Some of the programming was aimed at South Saint Paul, but most of it was for the metro area.

Our format, polka and country-Western, was distinctly different from any other station in the Twin Cities. As our station identification, we had customized singing jingles by the Schmidt Sisters, a very poular singing duo at the time. They sang the ID to the melody of Eddy Arnold's "Cattle Call": "Oooh, oooh, double-u-cow."

We called ourselves "the polka station at the top of the nation." A polka radio station in New Ulm, Minn., wasn't happy about us calling ourselves that, but South Saint Paul was further north than New Ulm, so I guess there wasn't anything they could do about it.

We had a free religious program, too—15 minutes every weekday. We invited local Protestant ministers and Catholic priests to participate—apparently there were no Jewish synagogues in South Saint Paul, because we never got a request from a rabbi to participate. Most of the clerics would come in and give a little sermon. At first a few Protestant ministers weren't happy that we divided it evenly between the Protestants and the Catholics, but eventually the novelty wore off and we had to beg the clergy to come to the station to do the show. We finally discontinued it due to lack of participation.

We announced with nicknames such as Arizona Al, Denver Don Doty (he became a big personality on WTCN, a top-of-the-line station), Buffalo Bob Montgomery (he went on to giant WCCO), Nevada Nick and Valley City Vic. We had 5,000 watts of power, which should be a darn good signal, but our dial location was poor—1590, right before 1600, the last location on the AM dial. On some radios you couldn't get us, but we drew a respectable audience.

Shortly after we started, KEYD in Golden Valley, 1440 on the dial, went country. It hired country personalities such as Johnny T and Texas Bill Strength. We hired Dave Dudley, a country-Western singer, to be an announcer. But his singing career was taking off and he left. He started with the Dave Dudley Trio in 1953; his biggest hit was "Six Days on the Road," which rose to number 2 on the country charts in 1963.

Texas Bill approached us about a job because, he said, he wasn't happy at KEYD. A contract was drawn up and Texas Bill signed it. But KEYD sued us to keep him. Had we given Bill even one dollar in the contract it would have been binding, but the contract didn't mention money. KEYD won their case and Texas Bill stayed put with an increase in pay.

Several years later, when I was on the City Council, I was asked to attend Texas Bill Strength's funeral. Some people were surprised to see me there. We were rivals, but only on the airwaves—I considered him a good friend.

WCOW was the first radio station to introduce rock 'n' roll and rhythm and blues in the Twin Cities market. One day in 1952 Joe Zingale, a young man just out of Bowling Green College, walked into WCOW looking for a job. He was from Cleveland and had no experience, but we took a liking to him. Besides, it was his first job, so we got him for little money.

He worked Sundays—a long shift from 8 A.M. to 8 P.M. Florence used to take him spaghetti every Sunday afternoon for supper. But he talked us into giving him his own radio show, and was replaced on Sundays by Mike Sirian, my boyhood friend. Mike had a good, secure job for the city of Saint

Paul, but he worked for us from time to time as he liked the additional income.

We gave Joe Saturday afternoons, I P.M. to 4 P.M. No country-Western for Joe—he played rock 'n' roll and rhythm and blues—the first DJ to do so in the Twin Cities. It became our number one show.

Joe stayed with us for a little more than a year, and we became very good friends. Florence and I went to Cleveland to meet his folks and they came to Saint Paul to spend time with my folks.

Joe went back to Cleveland and eventually bought a radio station in Atlantic City on borrowed money. He became a multi-millionaire, owning several big radio stations and the New Orleans Jazz (now the Utah Jazz) of the National Basketball Association. He finally ended up in the wholesale-diamond business. He lives in Ohio and has a villa and wine company in Italy.

He started with nothing. Couldn't happen to a nicer guy.

Sister Elizabeth Kenny, who was impressing people nationwide with her physical therapy for polio victims at the Sister Kenny Institute in the Twin Cities, was an interview guest on WCOW. We were very new on the air so we were happy to have her. Also on WCOW we had Frankie Yankovic, the polka king, who "tailor-made" radio spots for us at no charge after he hit it off with my brother Al. We would go to Schlief's Little City or the Medina Ballroom to hear him play.

One of WCOW's announcers, Dean Johnson, eventually made the mistake I knew would come sooner or later when we were promoting Schlief's. "Tonight at Schlief's Little Shitty, Frankie Yankovic," he announced one day.

Around the Dial

Around the Dial

NICK, AL, I AND PAPA WERE MAKING a living at WCOW. Papa was our maintenance man. He kept the place clean and was our go-fer, running errands. He liked to say he was the best paid handyman in Minnesota—and we brothers liked to hear it.

We were building additional successful radio stations—WKLJ in Sparta, Wis., and WKLK in Cloquet, Minn.

We bought the WKLJ license from the Rice family in the early 1950s and built the station. We made the national news when a vandal cut the guy wires for the tower, toppling it. The station always showed a profit, and eventually "Pinkie" Rice of the Rice family bought WKLJ from us.

WKLK in Cloquet was a bit frustrating because even though we covered Duluth with a good signal, we couldn't seem to capitalize on advertising. That was probably because Duluth had too many stations.

We did whatever we could to keep our advertisers happy. One Saturday afternoon brother Al called me at 3 P.M. to say that one of our clients, a nightclub in Carlton, Minn., was in a jam. Their band quit without notice and they couldn't find a replacement. By 9 P.M. I and the Tischler brothers were on the stage ready to go. I think we got $25 each, not bad for 1950, but 300 miles roundtrip—was it worth it? I don't think so, but of course I did it to help the station.

In 1950, the brothers, plus our dad, built the most successful station of the 13 Nick or I ever owned—KDUZ, Hutchinson, Minn.

The station got off to a fast start. Business was good—more business than at WCOW with half the staff. Al had recently married and chose to go manage KDUZ, where his new wife became very active in the operation. She was a beautiful model, and an intelligent one. But the views of Al and his bride and the views of Nick and I did not coincide. Al gave up his 25 percent of stock in WCOW for the 75 percent of KDUZ stock owned by Nick, me and Papa. Al's bride became 50 percent owner of all their stations. She played an important part in his success!!

At WCOW, Nick and I changed almost everything in 1960. We went for catchy call letters, WISK. The format became big band, and the frequency became 630, a much better spot on the AM dial for our 5,000 watts than 1590. The coverage was second only to WCCO, the radio giant of the Northwest.

And we were joined by Franklin Hobbs, who later became a big name as WCCO's all-night host. His entrance to Twin Cities radio was through my brother and I. We both took a big pay cut to afford Hobbs. He stayed with us at WISK six weeks—long enough to make a deal with WCCO, the 50,000-watt giant. We really feel he used us, but there wasn't anything we could do about it.

We tried our hand at different businesses to try to stabilize our income. Most were successful in the short haul, but eventually fizzled.

We started Statewide Sewing Machine Co. on East Seventh Street near Forest Street in Saint Paul. We sold a lot of sewing machines and put a great deal of radio business on WISK. But that lasted only about a year. Roxy Furniture, on East Seventh Street near Minnehaha Avenue, would have been successful if one of us had wanted to work there full time. But neither Nick nor I wanted to be tied down in a furniture store 10 to 12 hours a day. We sold it in the fall of 1961, and the buyers continued to advertise with us.

At WISK, we started a giveaway of Gift House Stamps in cooperation with sponsoring merchants. They were similar to S&H Green Stamps. It was an extremely successful promotion—we gave away thousands of the stamps, it kept us afloat and got us good listenership. But in the end, it benefited someone else, as we were getting into serious financial problems.

Nick and I were woefully underfinanced at WISK. Maybe we had moved along too quickly in acquiring and/or building radio stations. Even though business on the new giant increased each month, it was not enough to handle our financial obligations. Creditors were at our door. Our debt exceeded $300,000 by the sad day that the sale of our pride and joy to Crowell-Collier became final. Their cost: $850,000.

Radio-station licenses were transferred by the FCC at a snail's pace in those days. This one took nine months. At the time of filing for transfer, the station was heavily in the red. The financial picture improved each month, and by the date of transfer approval, the station was just in the black. If we had been able to own WISK another year, we could have taken care of our financial obligations. But there was nothing we could do—we had to sell.

It was the saddest day of our radio careers.

CHAPTER 38

The Next Guy's Formula for Success

CROWELL-COLLIER CHANGED THE CALL LETTERS to KDWB. They were big-time operators. Unbeknownst to most of the area station managers, KDWB was being promoted on their competitors' air without the competitors realizing it. Crowell-Collier had placed ads everywhere for "Formula 63," a make-you-feel-well elixir coming soon to your drug store. Only there was no Formula 63 and it wasn't coming to a drug store, it was a radio station and it was coming to the airwaves at 630 on the AM dial.

Crowell-Collier fooled everyone. The first day of operation, in the fall of 1961, KDWB played "Charlie Brown," the frenetic 1959 rock 'n' roll classic by the Coasters, continuously for 24 hours. That got the public's attention.

The station made its mark quickly. Too bad we didn't have that acumen. Within six months, KDWB became the number one station in the Twin Cities.

CHAPTER 39

The Personnel Parade

Nᴉᴄᴋ ᴀɴᴅ I ᴡᴇʀᴇ ɪɴ ᴀɴᴅ ᴏᴜᴛ of 13 radio stations during the 25-year span of our broadcast careers. We went on many trips from North Dakota to Ohio looking at towns with a population of 5,000 to 10,000 but without a radio station. Almost every town we visited and thought would be able to support a radio station eventually got one.

One of our better stations was KWEB in Rochester, Minn. Its format was rock 'n' roll. One Christmas a stuffy old bank president told us how much he liked "Jingle Bell Rock."

A minor crisis erupted at KWEB the time we engaged rock star Jerry Lee Lewis for a promotional concert at the Rochester Auditorium. But we hadn't hired a union pit band. The union was going to picket the show. Fortunately, I was a union musician and and I knew another union musician, Frank Evangelist, an excellent sax man who lived in Rochester. Frank put a band together, including me, and we were in the pit while Jerry Lee was on stage, pounding his piano through tunes like "Whole Lot of Shakin' Goin' On" and "Great Balls of Fire." If I remember correctly, we didn't even play one song. Just had to be there— union rules.

Nick and I encountered every type of individual. Trustworthy, productive, loyal employees such as Joe Zingale at WCOW. Sam Sabaen, known as Sam Sherwood, a tremendous asset to our organization at WCOW, became a number one disc jockey with KDWB. Don Johnson, our program director at WISK in Saint

Paul, later went to the same job at KFNF Shenandoah, Iowa, and then on to become one of the most popular DJs in Las Vegas.

We must have hired more than a thousand employees over the years. Many were great; others were not.

One of our stations was in a town big enough to support it, but the balance sheet wasn't showing it. The station should have been doing more business. In addition, the manager and the secretary were cruising the Mississippi River many afternoons. Nick and I just knew something was wrong.

I hired a woman to listen to the station from sign-on to sign-off and keep a log of all advertising time. The station's radio log did not jibe with the findings of the woman's log. She recorded more advertising business than the radio station had.

Nick and I found that the general manager and the secretary were in cahoots to cook the books to their advantage. We fired both of them, and the manager's father repaid us the thousands of dollars defrauded by his son to keep him out of jail. The son left town.

My brother Albert's operations were more successful than ours. He would say publicly to his managers, "I don't mind if you steal—leave a little bit for me." At one of our stations, our manager was running a successful radio station, though we noticed that every time we visited his house, we would see a new appliance or new piece of furniture.

Another manager said he could "sell sand to Egyptians." But I said to Nick—can he sell radio time? He couldn't. His stay with us was short.

CHAPTER 40

The Perks

W<small>E NEVER MADE ANY "BIG MONEY"</small> in the radio biz. But we had a lot of perks. We could stay at the Dunes Hotel in Las Vegas—rooms, dining and shows, all expenses paid through an exchange: the hotel services for free advertising on our radio station. The general manager took a liking to Florence, so we got extra-good service.

Florence and I met a lot of celebrities in our travels. In the early 1950s, we got first-class treatment from Bob Crosby on his afternoon television show in Hollywood. I gave one of the ushers one of my business cards, and soon we were invited in front of the cameras to talk with Bob "over the back fence," his gimmick for talking to guests. Maybe he chose us because he thought my card said WCCO, the television station that carried his program, not WCOW-South Saint Paul radio.

Another time, at Disneyland with the kids in the early 1960s, we met Jane Russell. She was there with a couple of little kids, and me, gutsy Vic, I say hello, how are you, I like your movies. She was really attractive and a very nice lady.

Also in the 1960s, we met Rosemary Clooney at the Coconut Grove nightclub in Hollywood. She was with her husband, José Ferrer. They chatted with us for some time—didn't fluff us off. About 2000, Florence and I met Miss Clooney again. This time she was in a Las Vegas show, "Four Girls Four" with Helen O'Connell and Margaret Whiting, who had been big band singers in the 1930s and 1940s, and Rose Marie, who was best-known for her supporting role on TV's "The Dick Van Dyke Show." Just as before Miss Clooney was so nice to us. Helen O'Connell was one of my favorites as a singer, but she wasn't friendly at all. Maybe she was having a bad day. Not all of us can be up at all times, but Rosemary Clooney was tops.

Yes, Nick and I enjoyed the radio business. Nick was an excellent time salesman. We hired so many people who conned us. But Nick always came out number one. I wasn't a good time salesman, I carried a little business. But I was good at management, programming, public relations and as contact person with the FCC in Washington, D.C.—but even I couldn't get the FCC to go along with our plans for KFNF in Shenandoah, Iowa.

CHAPTER 41

Doubling Our Gross
and Losing Money

Aꜰᴛᴇʀ ꜱᴇʟʟɪɴɢ WISK ɪɴ 1959, Nick and I moved to a small office in the First Merchants Bank Building at East Seventh and Minnehaha Streets in Saint Paul. Papa retired.

Our big Twin Cities radio presence was gone, but Nick and I still had to oversee our other stations, including KFNF in Shenandoah, Iowa, and KWKY in Des Moines.

We had formed a corporation, Tedesco, Inc., to buy KWKY with the help of stock we sold to some investors. It was the only station we didn't own outright.

KWKY was a second-tier radio station in Des Moines. It did OK financially, thanks to a good manager, Walt Martel. Now it is a full-time religious station and doing very well financially.

We bought KFNF station in 1960. Shenandoah was a sleepy town in southwest Iowa where nothing much happens, though Nick and I livened up the place when we hired the rock band Jefferson Airplane, now Jefferson Starship, to perform at the armory. Unlike the Jerry Lee Lewis shows in Rochester, which made a profit, the Jefferson Airplane show in Shenandoah barely broke even.

Still, Nick and I did have at least one special night in Shenandoah. We were staying at the Tall Corn Motel when we ran into Milburn Stone and Ken Curtis. The stars of the very popular TV show "Gunsmoke," who played "Doc" and "Festus," respectively, were in town for a Page County Fair appearance. We got

One of the perks of radio life was meeting celebrities. In Shenandoah, Iowa,
I spent a wonderful time with Ken Curtis, left, and Milburn Stone,
who played "Festus" and "Doc," respectively, on TV's "Gunsmoke."

to talking—they were regular guys—and went to dinner with
them, had our picture taken with them. We never saw each other
again.

KFNF was founded in 1922, one of the first radio stations in
the nation. Its call letters meant "keeping friendliness next to
the farmer," and in its earliest days was owned by a strong company, Henry Field Seed Co. By the time we got to Shenandoah,
the number one station in town was KMA, founded in 1924 and
owned by the May Seed Co.

Nick and I had known that two radio stations in a town of
6,000 people didn't make sense. We had bought KFNF with
the intention of moving it to Council Bluffs, Iowa, to serve the
market across the Missouri River—Omaha, Neb., an audience of
more than a million people. In Shenandoah, the audience was
fewer than 100,000 listeners.

When we bought KFNF, we were only grossing $6,000 a month but we were netting $2,000 a month. Our station manager was Don Johnson from WISK. When he left for a better arrangement, we made our office secretary the temporary manager. She ran a tight ship with a small staff.

We then hired a manager with great credentials from Dayton, Ohio. He wanted to upgrade the station, so we joined the ABC Radio network about 1963. We carried the Kansas City Athletics baseball games and the Kansas City Chiefs football games. Our ads and listenership increased.

We doubled our monthly gross to $12,000—but we were losing $2,000 a month.

We let the contracts with ABC, the Athletics and the Chiefs expire by 1964. We liked the manager but he wasn't heading in the same direction as we were, and he resigned. Once again we appointed the office manager to run the station. The gross fell, but KFNF became profitable again.

We kept petitioning the FCC to move KFNF to Council Bluffs, but our attempts were futile. I believe several powerhouse radio stations put political pressure on the FCC to keep us out of Omaha. The FCC concluded our service was more needed in Shenandoah than Council Bluffs-Omaha. We sold KFNF in 1965.

There are still two stations in Shenandoah. However, KFNF's successor is a completely religious station, like KWKY in Des Moines, and, I hear, very profitable.

— CHAPTER 42 —

All the News That's Fit
about Football

IN 1964 NICK SPENT THE WINTER in Florida while I tended
the company store at the First Merchant Bank Building. But
with ownership of only KFNF and KWKY, there wasn't much to
attend to—other than a few disgruntled stockholders in Tedesco,
Inc., complaining about the value of their stock, the phone didn't
ring much.

With time on my hands, I embarked on a new venture—
publishing a tabloid sports newspaper called *Touchdown USA*.

I was not much of a sportsman, though I did go hunting one fall
in the late 1950s with some friends since boyhood, Joe DiSanto,
Chris Santori and "Turk" Minnelli. I shot a pheasant and I really
felt bad. It was my first and only hunt. I gave my shotgun to Walt
Martel, our station manager at KWKY in Des Moines.

But I had been a longtime football fan, and the Minnesota
Vikings, an expansion franchise of the National Football League,
had brought increased awareness of professional football when
they came to town in 1960.

In the 1950s, Father Tom Meagher of Catholic Charities used
to arrange NFL exhibition games in town. The fund-raisers
were held at what is now known as Griffin Stadium, capacity
about 6,000 people, at Central High School, Saint Paul. The
first pro football team I ever saw play was the New York Giants
when Joe Fercello and I attended one of Father Tom's games,
but I don't remember if it was in 1953 against Green Bay or

96

in 1955 against Baltimore. Father Tom did as much as anyone to keep football interest alive in the Twin Cities until the pros got here.

At the time, the NFL and the American Football League were fierce competitors. Minnesota was first awarded an AFL franchise, but owner-to-be Max Winter turned it down to hold out for the NFL.

I hired Bob Utecht of Twin Cities hockey fame as the editor; Roger Rosenblum of the *Saint Paul Dispatch-Pioneer Press* to cover the Minnesota Vikings; Lee Remel, a sportswriter with a Green Bay paper, for the Packers; and a top sports reporter from each NFL and AFL city to cover its team. The teams in the AFL cities were much more cooperative with my newspaper because they were the new guys and wanted the publicity.

I was fortunate to get Otto Graham, the great quarterback for the Cleveland Browns in the 1950s, to write a one-time column, as well as Bill Russell, basketball ace for the Boston Celtics to do likewise.

As publisher of a football paper, I had full access to the Vikings locker room throughout the week and, on game day, the sidelines.

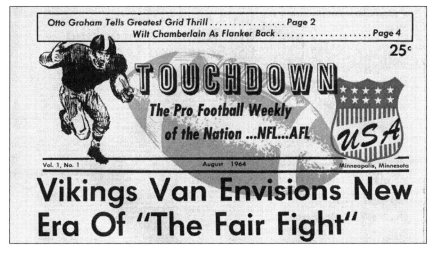

Volume 1, Number 1 of *Touchdown USA*. I only published 11 issues before it went bust.

Norm Van Brocklin, coach at the time, would give his players hell in the locker room—and lace the hell with racial slurs. I became good friends with him—I knew he was a Civil War buff, so from time to time I'd give him a book on the subject. That did it.

The Vikings played outdoors in Metropolitan Stadium in Bloomington, just south of Minneapolis. On a beautiful fall Sunday afternoon, there wasn't anywhere nicer to be. Even the cold, snowy winter afternoons were filled with excitement and I didn't mind the weather. I couldn't believe I had the right to follow the game on the sidelines. Up and down the field I'd go.

Publishing football news gave me something in common with football greats around the country. My favorite player at home, the nicest guy on the Vikings, was Carl Eller, recently voted into the NFL Hall of Fame. He and I both graduated from Metropolitan State University, but at different times.

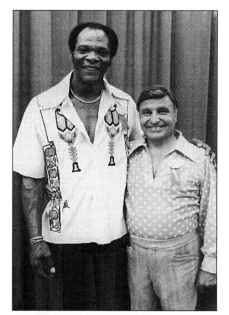

I met Green Bay Packers Coach Vince Lombardi in Las Vegas. We talked for at least 15 minutes. I asked him if he thought the NFL and AFL would merge. He said if they didn't, it would bankrupt the league. The players' salaries were skyrocketing, and the competitive battle was a financial strain on both leagues. They merged in 1967.

One day I was walking down the street in Washington, D.C., when along came a guy shuffling a football from one hand to the other. I think he did it so people would know who he was. I said, "Hey, you're Jim Brown." The star of the

Carl Eller of the Vikings was a giant of a man, and not just physically. He was my favorite Vikings player. We posed for this picture about 1985.

Cleveland Browns was most gracious as we stopped to talk, and I really think he was happy that I recognized him. But if it hadn't been for the football, I don't think I would have.

I also got to go to parties. I met and had my picture taken with George Halas, owner of the Chicago Bears, Coach Van Brocklin and others. I was in seventh heaven. There was Y. A. Tittle, quarterback for the New York Giants; Paul Flatley, stand-out rookie wide receiver in 1963 for the Minnesota Vikings; Father Tom Meagher of Catholic Charities; Pete Rozelle, NFL Commissioner; Ed Martini, manager of the Vikings, and Ray Mock of the Minnesota Minutemen, an organization dedicated to promoting professional sports in Minnesota.

I still have their pictures in my office. I also have 11 issues of *Touchdown USA*—all that I was able to publish.

Because of my radio contacts, I had been able to obtain some advertisers. I had Merit Chevrolet, thanks to my brother Nick's strong association with Merit owner Chris Rinkel, and I had Shoppers City, thanks to Mel Roth, general manager and CEO, who also was a major investor in WISK radio. I struck a trade arrangement with the Thunderbird Motel and restaurant—they paid for their print advertisements with $250 a month in free meals and rooms, and my family made good use of that arrangement.

The advertising in *Touchdown USA* was strong at first, but I couldn't follow it up with circulation. I got some free advertising on sports programs on the Mutual Broadcasting System, but that brought us fewer than 100 subscribers. Some of the local radio and TV stations gave us exposure. But that only brought us up to about 1,000 subscribers.

Supposedly I had an arrangement with the Vikings to introduce our sports paper to their season-ticket holders with a free mailing. Somewhere, something went wrong. I had thousands of newspapers printed, but they didn't get out. The people in the Vikings organization kept passing the buck as to who had made the original agreement. They definitely let me down. To this day I feel betrayed.

The debts became too much for me to handle. After 11 issues,

I sold the paper for $1.00 plus obligations to *TV Times,* a popular TV listing paper. That publisher produced four issues before the paper was put to sleep.

Several years later, Bob Lurtsema, a popular former Vikings player, started *Viking Update,* a similar publication, which became successful. Maybe he had access to the Vikings ticket holders to pull it off.

CHAPTER 43

Back to the Beat

My time with *Touchdown USA* made me feel quite important and fortunate. It would have been a great way to make a living.

But my association with pro football withered away after the tabloid folded. Back to the uncertainty of radio income and not knowing what tomorrow would bring, I went back to playing nightclubs with my three- or four-piece band called Vic Tedoo and his Jazzy Crew, a name tabbed on us by Bill Schneider, at the time probably the best drummer in Saint Paul, whose day job was as a promotional department manager at the *Saint Paul Dispatch-Pioneer Press.*

Later I became known as "Saxy Vic" Tedoo. Saxy, yes. Sexy, no!!

This family portrait is my treasure. I had to be talked into sitting for it, and I'm so glad I agreed because Elizabeth died unexpectedly not too long afterward, early in 2001. Florence and I are seated, with the kids between us, from left, Elizabeth, Tony and Patricia.

Our daughter Patricia made us so happy when she gave birth to our first grandchild, Justin, born in 1977. We posed for a four-generation picture: from left are my mother, Aïda Tedesco; my daughter, Patricia Tedesco Bloyer; her son, Justin Bloyer; and me, Vic Tedesco.

Election signs for Tedesco were a common sight in Saint Paul for many years.

My council office was a colorful sight each Christmas
when I displayed greeting cards from constituents.

I'm more in love with my wife now than ever.
This is my favorite picture of Florence.

My grandson, Justin Bloyer,
is an airline pilot.

My granddaughter, Kirstin Bloyer,
is just beginning her career.

Donna Jayne Safford
did a great job as the manager
of a wig shop owned by me
and my City Council deputy,
John Ricci.

Mayor Larry Cohen, right, made everything about
the mayor's job look easy. Here we posed with Mel
Blanc, the voice of animated rabbit Bugs Bunny,
during his visit to Saint Paul in the early 1970s.

I'll never forget Mary Tyler Moore. She was so kind to me and my son, Tony, during a 1970s visit in Minneapolis.

Walter Mondale is probably my favorite politician—a swell guy who didn't forget you.

What a cold day, but what an honor to ride on Minnesota's float in the inaugural parade for President Jimmy Carter, Jan. 20, 1977. That's me in the front in the short pants.

I was a late starter when it came to a college education,
graduating at age 55 from Metropolitan State University in Saint Paul.

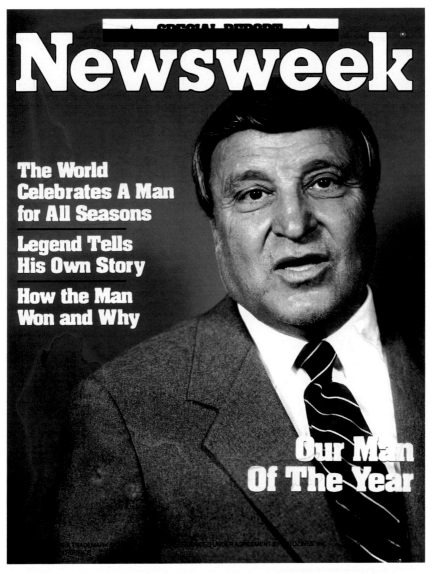

Newsweek

**The World
Celebrates A Man
for All Seasons**

**Legend Tells
His Own Story**

**How the Man
Won and Why**

**Our Man
Of The Year**

I had so much fun with this fake Newsweek cover. I took it to the
Council chambers, where my colleagues reacted with awe.

What wonderful years I had on the City Council. Jerry Fearing of the
Saint Paul Pioneer Press-Dispatch drew me many times over the years,
and I especially like the "sad note" cartoon he drew when I retired.

PART FOUR

People-Pleasing Politics

CHAPTER 44

It Started as a Lark

I ADMIT I WAS DOWN AND ALMOST OUT. I had failed in the publishing business and had no real "day job." I had only a couple of radio stations to look after, and that didn't take much.

Several days after Christmas 1965, State Rep. Richard Richie and Fiori Palarine, a prominent lawyer from the Iron Range who practiced in Saint Paul, called on me. They wanted me to run for City Council.

I was shocked and said "no way." I felt overwhelmed. I had no experience, and I knew it cost money to promote oneself.

The three of us went up to the Lamb's Club, a neighborhood bar and restaurant. They explained that St. Paul was predominantly Irish and German, with only folks of Irish and German descent on the council. They thought a councilman of Italian descent should represent them. After several martinis, I agreed to run.

It started out as a lark for me. My first step toward an endorsement was with my peers, the Italian-American Voters Educational League. Richie, Palarine and I felt the endorsement was automatic, but it wasn't. As in most clubs, you had a few dissenters, and the endorsement was to be voted on two weeks later.

Very few of them wanted more time to check me out. Most of them had known me for 42 years—I don't know what else they had to check out. It was just stalling tactics on the part of two or three members who apparently didn't like me. I was disappointed the club didn't vote the matter up or down immediately, but I could see most of them did not want to rock the boat.

The next step was to go before the DFL nominating committee. I was quite apprehensive because of my encounter at the Italian-American Voters League. Several of the endorsements had been automatic, such as those for council veterans such as Robert Peterson and Bernard Dalglish, but three of us appeared in front of the committee, whose members asked courteous but tough questions. I was comfortable before them. And I was nominated to go before the DFL convention for endorsement.

Harry Marshall later told me what clinched it for me was that I said I intended to run for office with or without their endorsement, and since I would be a strong candidate, I would probably knock off one of their endorsed candidates in the primary.

CHAPTER 45

The Politics of All-Nighters

THE BATTLE FOR ENDORSEMENT at the DFL convention was quite contentious and I got my first taste of politics.

Six council seats were up for grabs. Robert Peterson, a long-time and well-respected councilman, was endorsed on the first ballot. Incumbents James Dalglish and Bud Holland made it on the second and Bill Carlson, veteran politico, on the third. The fifth ballot brought endorsement to Severin Mortinson, a Republican incumbent who had been defeated in the previous City Council election but was coming back to life as a Democrat.

That left one spot open for three hopeful candidates: George McMahon, a union favorite; Chris Durand, one of the earliest African-Americans to seek a council seat; and me. The ballots went on and on and none of us three could get the 51 percent necessary for nomination.

About 2:30 in the morning, Karl Grittner, a state senator at the time, stood up and said we're deadlocked, let's go with a five-party slate instead of six. Mary Lou Klas, who later became a federal judge, got up and said, "No, we don't, Karl. We stayed till 2:30 A.M. when you were nominated for state senator, and we're not going home till we endorse."

I won the endorsement on the next ballot by one vote.

I was later told I was short two-three votes and a couple of the party faithful doing the counting said it was inevitable that I would be endorsed, so why not let everyone go home?

After the DFL endorsed me, the Italian-American Voters Educational League endorsed me on an automatic and unanimous vote!!

CHAPTER 46

"Vote Tedesco"

CAMPAIGNING WAS A NEW AND EXCITING life for me. Our campaign was energetic, the talk of all.

I needed and welcomed support from such people as R. William Reilly, Mae and Leroy Benshoof, Irene and Harold Speak, Don Ferrin, Saint Paul city attorney Joe Summers, Richard Radman, John L. Ricci, Mary Lou Klas, Larry and Rose May, and my sister and brother-in-law, Alfred and Mary Gentile.

Florence and the kids helped, too. Elizabeth, 13, and Tony, 10, were attending grade school at Saint Pascal's and Patricia was 16, in high school at Hill-Murray. They stuffed and mailed political pieces. The rest of us went to block parties, neighborhood meetings, political clubs, League of Women Voters, etc. We made them all.

Then there were phone banks. Joe Lombardo, a supporter of mine and the owner of State Supply at East Seventh Street and Payne Avenue, let us use his eight phone lines each night. It was amazing the amount of support my campaign was receiving.

Harold Speak and Don Ferrin designed my political yard signs, which were yellow and green—so different from the staid red, white and blue. And Bunky Caliguire, the guy who threw his cap at me at Camp Stoneman? He was my sign campaign manager. He put the signs up and did an excellent job. The locations were established by the calling of the phone bank for approval.

Only two Italian families would not let me put my political-campaign signs in their yards. One was Jimmy Falbo, my good friend back in Little Italy days.

At the start of my first political campaign, Florence and I sat for a family portrait with the kids, from left, Patricia, 16, Tony, 10, and Elizabeth, 13.

This all took money. I was in the thick of battle to be elected and I lent my campaign committee $2,500—quite a hefty sum in 1966. And on primary day at R. William Reilly's suggestion, we had several air balloons that said "Vote Tedesco" flying over the loop of Saint Paul. Our signs were the only ones that read "vote," not "elect" or "re-elect." This was quite novel at the time and generated a lot of positive conversation.

It was an extremely successful primary campaign. I ran third out of 27 candidates.

CHAPTER 47

The Immigrants' Son Gets Elected

Twelve candidates survived the primary to compete for the six open council seats.

The DFL slate of six candidates was Peterson, Dalglish, Holland, Carlson, Mortinson and Tedesco.

Several members in the DFL Party wanted me to be the "hatchet man," i.e., that is, the candidate who would get into personal squabbles with opposing candidates. But my election-savvy committee people said, "No way." That job went to Mortinson, the only one of the DFLers who didn't get elected.

I waited for results on Election Night at DFL headquarters, which was upstairs in an old building near the Seven Corners area of Saint Paul. The top six vote-getters would be on the council. Mortinson, the hatchet man, didn't make the cut. I ran fourth out of the 12. I was in.

As soon as the results were in, I immediately left DFL headquarters to go to my dad's house, accompanied by my wife, Florence, and Doug Locke, a supporter of mine. (Funny, even though I liked Doug, I never saw him again.)

My papa brought out the "dago red" wine and we celebrated. More than 50 years earlier, he had left behind his family in Italy to find a better life in America. And there was Mama, who had to wait seven years before her husband could afford to pay for the family's journey across an ocean and halfway across a continent.

How proud my parents were of me. I always tried, in my 21-plus years in politics, not to do anything that would damage their pride in me.

CHAPTER 48

The Work Begins

Some of my constituents in Little Italy compared me to the "Little Flower"—not Saint Theresa of Lisieux, but Fiorello LaGuardia, the colorful, diminutive mayor of New York City from 1934 to 1945.

He was the first Italian-American mayor of New York; I was the second Italian-American elected to the St. Paul City Council, after Frank Marzitelli. LaGuardia read the comics to the kids on Sunday morning radio in New York during a newspaper strike; in the '40s I was reading comics to the kids on radio station WSHB in Stillwater. And there was a physical resemblance—we were both short, dark-haired Italians. Could it be that I had unconsciously followed in the political footsteps of Mayor LaGuardia?

We were elected in April 1966. The hoopla, the handshakes and the well-wishing were over, and it was time to get to work.

Even before I was sworn in, my little office on the east side of Saint Paul was a busy place. I was besieged with constituents wanting this or that. I remember a Mrs. Jackson, who wanted me to reopen Cayuga Playgrounds. She was a nice woman and dedicated to her cause, but she drove me crazy. I could see political life was going to be busy.

Tom Byrne was the new mayor, a class guy. He was a kind, gentle man who did his job in a steady style. He wasn't looking for a spotlight.

At the time I was first elected, each City Council member was a commissioner, with responsibility for a certain department of the city, such as Public Works or Police and Public Safety. When Byrne met with us to make council assignments, I told him I preferred the Department of Libraries, the easiest assignment of them all. I certainly did not want the Department of Parks and Recreation, a hotbed of neighborhood pressure and politics. You guessed it—I got Parks and Rec.

It turned out to be a blessing. I guess the best six years of my life were as commissioner of Parks and Recreation.

From my earliest months in office, I caused trouble. Cartoonist Jerry Fearing drew me and Mayor Tom Byrne in August 1966.

CHAPTER 49

In the Flow at the Parks

POLITICS WAS MY THIRD CAREER, after music and broadcasting. All three are distinctively different, but they have one common denominator—people-pleasing. I was promotional-minded, and that fit the Parks and Rec job.

In fact, I was a perfect match for the position. Things started to fall into place. I was in charge of 18 park police, 40 staff members at Como Zoo and many building inspectors and park staff members—overall, a staff of more than 300 people.

Building inspectors and park staff were an odd mix to be supervising, but the two had been put together long before I became parks commissioner. The blending, called the Department of Parks, Recreation and Public Buildings, was done to add fund-raising clout for the commissioner at re-election time—many building owners could be included on the invitation list for fund-raising events.

Of all the council members, I seemed to be the best one to be in charge of playgrounds, and I really got involved with them, along with John Ricci, my extremely competent assistant. I got to know the recreation directors by name. I got along well with the kids; I played softball with them. Eventually, I was even able to reopen Cayuga Playgrounds.

The country was going through tough economic times in 1966. President Lyndon Johnson was talking about wage guidelines to keep inflation down. In St. Paul, Mayor Byrne wanted all of us department heads to find ways to save money. We looked at very serious trims that year and in succeeding years, such as

I took a few swings on the ball diamond during the late 1960s when I was Parks commissioner. The catcher was John Ricci, my deputy commissioner.

the possibility of closing playgrounds and laying off staff for a week or two. But that first summer as parks commissioner, I had a lot of fun at Como Park one night while saving the city $7.

Tom Flynn conducted the community sings on Wednesday nights at Como's Lakeside Pavilion. He was unhappy with the $18 he got for each show. He wanted more dough—I said no!! I replaced him—I led the community sing one Wednesday in July. About a thousand people were there as I led off with "Side by Side."

The newspapers wanted a picture of me and some ladies singing. I found two sweet old ladies instead of some swingin' chicks. My strongest constituency was senior citizens. I had been entertaining gratis for years at government-owned high-rises in the city, and I didn't forget church groups either—wherever seniors would gather.

Don Del Fiacco, writer for the *Dispatch-Pioneer Press,* did a nice story on me. Pete Hohn was there from the *Minneapolis Tribune,* taking a picture and doing a write-up.

Flynn had wanted $25 per performance, so when I replaced him at $18, I saved the city $7. I donated my fee to the parks' booster clubs. Even though I was a hit, my tenure as song leader at Como lasted only one engagement. Tom Flynn agreed to a

compromise raise of $2—well above President Johnson's wage guideline of 3.2 percent—and returned at $20 a performance.

The $7 wasn't much money, but I did show that I was able to tackle a problem with "profound alacrity."

I had fun with that term during my political career and ever since. It was a term that Ed Hedfelt, department head of the Housing Authority, beat to death. Most people, upon hearing

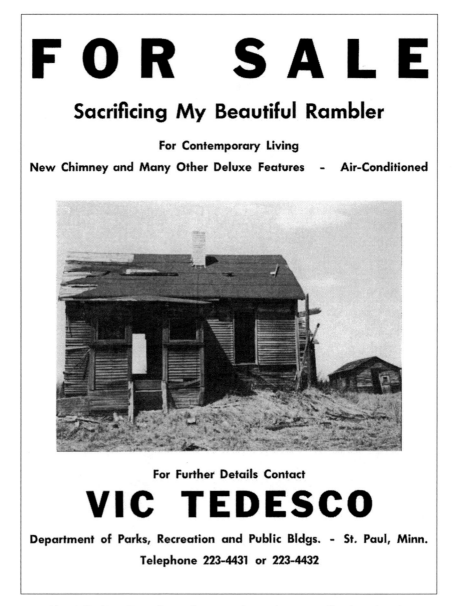

FOR SALE

Sacrificing My Beautiful Rambler

For Contemporary Living

New Chimney and Many Other Deluxe Features   -   Air-Conditioned

For Further Details Contact

VIC TEDESCO

Department of Parks, Recreation and Public Bldgs. - St. Paul, Minn.

Telephone 223-4431 or 223-4432

About the time I condemned my own house in a council vote set up by
city attorney Joe Summers, I distributed a "for sale" joke.

him, would say, "What did he say?" I learned it meant "move swiftly."

Almost all the work involving the parks was fun; almost all the work on the City Council was routine. To offset that, once in a while we would pull a prank on each other.

One day in 1966 the council was voting on resolutions condemning houses—usually routine stuff. I stepped out of the chamber for a bit and when I got back I kept signing papers for the different addresses to be condemned. I wasn't paying close attention, so I had no qualms about signing a paper to condemn a house described as "deteriorated and dilapidated and in need of paint," that the interior "was littered and a possible fire hazard" and that it was a "possible hangout for undesireables."

Unfortunately, the address of that house was my own—1667 Conway St.

I was the laughingstock of that session when the joke came out. It was the work of city attorney Joe Summers, a brilliant lawyer and one of my political supporters. He later became one of the first co-hosts of "Almanac" with Jan Smaby, a political show on Twin Cities public television.

CHAPTER 50

The Profit Stops Here

THE COUNCIL MEMBER WHO HAD BEEN the previous parks commissioner, Frank Loss, had plastered his name on signs at all the Parks and Rec centers. I had his name painted out with black paint and did not put up new signs with my name on them. After several years, the paint wore off and when his name reappeared, some people actually thought he had been reelected.

But the influence of Commissioner Loss lingered in other ways. He had leased Newell Park, a small park in Midway, for $1 a year to a private group, the Snelling Avenue Commercial Club. Reliable sources told me they had stag parties, girlie shows, card games and crap games amongst the club members. The club also was renting out the park pavilion at a considerable profit for weddings and private parties.

One night in December 1966 I went to the park, at Hewitt and Fairview Avenues, just west of Snelling Avenue, accompanied by Larry May and several buddies of his. May, the finance

In January 1969 I posed on a ski jump to promote skiing in Saint Paul parks. In time I became a good-enough skier.

chairman for my campaign, was a big guy, 6 foot 4, and his two buddies also were big guys. Inside the park pavilion there was a card game going on, and beer and plenty of smoke. The group didn't pay any attention to me. Even though they knew who I was, it was like I didn't exist. But they soon found that I did.

I terminated their lease. I gave them 30 days' notice to get out. The group resisted for several months, but in the end the club vacated the park. The group ended up paying big rent for space on Snelling Avenue near University. I can't express my gratitude enough to Larry May and his friends for accompanying me that night.

Newell Park was restored to what the taxpayers were paying for: a city park. And I was enjoying what would turn out to be the six happiest years of my life.

CHAPTER 51

Kicking the Status Quo . . .

THE PRESS WAS GOOD TO ME OVER the Newell incident. The *Saint Paul Pioneer Press* and the *Saint Paul Dispatch* both gave me a lot of ink, including, in the *Dispatch*, a Jerry Fearing cartoon of me kicking the businessmen's group out of the park. I continued to look for ways to improve the city's ways of handling the parks.

Florence, at left, and I were chaperones in the late 1960s for the Junior Royalty coronation of the Saint Paul Winter Carnival. Also attending the royalty was son Tony, left, dressed as a page.

One of the biggest events of the year in Saint Paul was the Winter Carnival, and one of the biggest events was the Junior Royalty coronation of the Parks and Recreation Department at the old Saint Paul Auditorium. Even though the event was free, we typically drew only 1,500 people, who looked lost in the big auditorium, which could seat 6,000 people.

Parks and Rec usually printed about 3,000 tickets, and they were distributed at every recreation center in town. The year I changed the status quo, I had 10,000 tickets printed, and we gave them away through senior citizen buildings, supermarkets, recreation centers and radio-station promotions.

I've always "played percentages" in my life. I knew we'd never get 10,000 people—at least, I hoped we wouldn't, because the auditorium wouldn't hold them all—but we did get 4,000, almost three times as much as previous houses.

CHAPTER 52

.... But Not Too Hard

ONE DAY AT MY OFFICE, a lawyer came in with two guys. They were tough-looking. With pinstripe suits and loud ties, they looked as if they had stepped out of a Jimmy Cagney gangster movie. I couldn't believe my ears: They wanted me to help them establish a house of ill repute. I was frightened by their presence, and so relieved when they left, and more so when I didn't see them again. I gave the attorney hell for bringing them to see me.

CHAPTER 53

I Talk to the Animals—
and the Animals Yap Back

IN MY EARLY YEARS ON THE COUNCIL, I never missed a photo op. Harking back to my misbehaving youth, a Saint Paul newspaper had me reenact getting my ears pulled by the priest who had been at Saint Ambrose, Father Pioletti, who was by then a monsignor.

I and the little cub both enjoyed Joan Embry of the San Diego Zoo,
who had come to visit Como Zoo in the late 1960s.

But most of the photos came from work with Como Zoo, which was one of my biggest responsibilities for Parks and Rec. The zoo staff and I got along well. They named a llama after me—Vic Dalama. Sounds Italian, doesn't it?

The zoo wasn't very big, but it was the darling of animal lovers throughout the area. John Fletcher, the zoo director, was a dedicated public servant. We had excellent rapport, maybe cause I spent more time at the zoo in one month than the previous commissioner had done in two years—his full term. That helped me be more attuned to what was going on at the zoo.

I was open to the establishment of a metropolitan zoo, which eventually came to pass as the Minnesota Zoo in Apple Valley. I felt the larger zoo, with paid admission, and Como, with free admission, would complement each other.

I met with Stanley Hubbard Sr., general manager and owner of KSTP-TV and AM and FM radio stations, to let him and others know I was in favor of the metro zoo. Many years earlier, in 1949, the year my brothers and I opened our first radio station, I was in the Gopher Grill of the Saint Paul Hotel with a group of radio broadcasters who said Stan Hubbard was perturbed because every Tom, Dick and Harry was getting in the broadcasting business. At the time there were 2,000 radio stations; today there are more than 10,000.

CHAPTER 54

A Match Made in Omaha

ONE OF THE BEST ATTRACTIONS at Como Zoo while I was Parks commissioner was Casey the gorilla. But Casey was lonely. He had no companion. So we made arrangements with the Henry Dorley Zoo in Omaha, Neb., to send Casey there to be teamed up with a female who was in need of a little fond affection.

One of the city's corporations lent us their Lear jet to transport Casey, me and several reporters to Omaha in 1969. Someone at the Saint Paul newspapers later told me that because it was near election time, they hadn't wanted to give me coverage, but because of the interest in Casey they felt they had to.

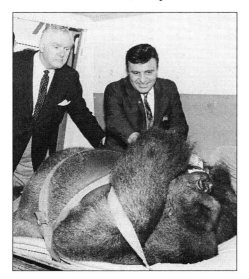

Poor Casey. Unlucky in love at Como Zoo, he got drugged and strapped for the ride to Omaha.

Casey was not in a cage for his jet ride; he was strapped and drugged and spent the trip sleeping on the floor in the rear of the plane. When we got to Omaha, he was transferred to a truck with a cage to be taken to the zoo.

We had an arrangement with Dorley to be given the first offspring and every other one thereafter. It took Casey a while to get interested, and then his first few offspring died, but eventually we were ready to receive a female, Tamoo.

When Arlene Scheunemann, a devoted Como docent, took Tamoo out of her crate the first time, I wanted to hold the little gorilla. I took her in my arms, she got a good grip on my hair, which was really a hairpiece, and it slid over my eyes. Flashbulbs popped.

Casey never came back to Como. Instead, John Fletcher looked for a pair of gorillas, and found them in Don and Donna.

CHAPTER 55

Bringing Up Baby

THE GORILLAS WHO CAME TO COMO in the ealy 1970s had been "wild-caught" in the jungles of Africa and brought to the United States by an animal dealer. It was later discovered that the hunters who found the two broke the law: They killed the babies' parents to get to the little ones. Nowadays, no zoo gorillas are wild-caught; they are all bred in captivity.

But there were the babies at Como, about a year old. They needed care, just as human babies would. Arlene Scheunemann gave that care, baby bottles and cribs and all. In an exception to the zoo's free-admission policy, we charged 10 cents to see the gorillas, but Tuesdays were free.

The two gorillas probably weren't siblings but because they had been brought up together they acted like brother and sister and never produced offspring. Don died in the early 1990s, established within an all-male group of gorillas. Before he passed away, Donna went on a breeding loan to a zoo in North Carolina. She didn't breed there either, but took on the role of an auntie to a family group of gorillas; she's still thriving in 2005.

I had named Don after Don Boxmeyer, a well-loved and respected news reporter for the Saint Paul papers. Donna was named after Donna Jayne Safford, the manager of a wig shop owned by me and John Ricci, my deputy commissioner.

CHAPTER 56

The Business of Hair

I HAD BEEN WEARING A HAIRPIECE since late 1965, and I got the idea to go into the wig business because I thought maybe I'd be happier paying wholesale for my pieces, which needed replacing about every year.

The wholesale cost for all wigs was $7 to $10, and you could sell them retail for $29.99 to $49.99. John Ricci and I opened up Donna Jayne's Wig Shoppe in the late 1960s at 1664 White Bear Ave., Saint Paul, in the Hillcrest Shopping Center.

Donna Jayne Safford was the manager. Next to my wife, Florence, Donna Jayne was the hardest working woman I ever met. She worked 10 to 12 hours a day, including weekends. The shop was doing great, but we got greedy. We opened a second store out in Stillwater at the Saint Croix Mall. It was beautiful, much nicer than the Hillcrest site, but the sales were anemic.

In seven months we sold both stores to Joe Francis. He closed the Stillwater store and added a beauty salon to the Hillcrest location, still in operation.

To this day John and I are grateful to Miss Safford for her hard work. If she had pressed us for overtime, I'm sure it would have been a tidy sum. But she did not. She was an honorable person and John and I held her in the highest regard.

I'm still wearing hairpieces, and paying retail not wholesale, and glad of it.

CHAPTER 57

And a Flip of the Wig to You

Some guys are very private about wearing a hairpiece, but I was not. I would use it to amaze little kids at the mayor's Christmas parties, of which I was the master of ceremonies.

Several thousand kids would attend, and I would ask them, "Hey, kids, do you want to see a magic trick?" They would yell yes, and I would flip off my hairpiece. You could see the looks of amazement on their faces.

On another occasion, a group of at least 50 Japanese men and women were visiting the City Council, and things were feeling quite formal, so I told their interpreter, a young lady from Saint Louis Park, to tell them that I was part Japanese. She told the visitors, and they began to smirk.

I looked at them and said, "My mother and father were from Italy, and my hair is from Japan," and flipped off my hairpiece.

They roared with laughter, and you could feel the stiffness leave the room.

Anytime I spoke as Parks commissioner in front of large groups of children, I was apt to flip my wig at them.

CHAPTER 58

Close Encounters of the Python Kind

Aɪᴛʜᴏᴜɢʜ I ʟᴏᴠᴇᴅ ᴛʜᴇ ᴘʜᴏᴛᴏ ᴏᴘs at the zoo, they had their problems. Once I had to hold a monkey, and it bit me. I had to go to Ramsey Hospital, now Regions, for stitches. In the late 1970s, another zoo animal bit me, Woscar the Wombat, but he didn't break the skin.

In January 1967, I was invited to the annual weigh-in of Julie, an 18-foot python snake, the kind that squeezes its prey to death. The weigh-ins were handled like this: A volunteer would step on the scales with the snake along for the ride. Weight of the two minus the weight of the volunteer equaled the weight of the snake.

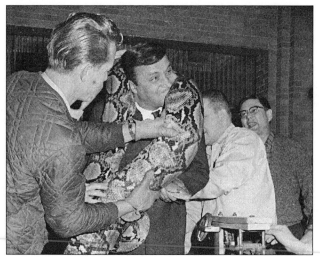

In 1967 at Como Zoo, Julie the python put a squeeze on me that was seen round the world. Zoo director John Fletcher is at right. Photo used by permission of Associated Press.

By 1978, I was more prudent about Julie. I was a mere spectator, second from left, when she weighed in at 138 pounds and 18 feet, 3 inches long.

So the staff wanted to drape Julie around me for the weigh-in—and news-hungry me, like a dummy, I agreed to it.

Soon Julie started to wrap herself around me. I was frightened to no end, the TV cameras were rolling, and I started to scream for help. It took eight people to pull her off me.

That evening I had to fly to Washington, D.C., on business. When I got off the plane at National Airport, there was the picture of me and the hungry snake on the front page of the afternoon newspaper, the *Washington Star.* The picture eventually was on the front page of *Stars and Stripes,* the servicemen's tabloid, too. Several magazines also ran it—calling me Paul Tedesco. The *Minneapolis Star* plus papers in Denver and Omaha ran cartoons, and Jerry Fearing drew me once again for the *Saint Paul Dispatch.*

CHAPTER 59

Trouble in the Third Round

T HEN THERE WAS THE BABY ELEPHANT I lent to the campaign staff of Stephen Maxwell, an African-American who later became a very popular judge. In 1966 he was a Republican candidate for Congress running against Joe Karth. His staff thought it would be fun to have an elephant, symbol of the GOP, at one of his political fund-raisers.

My fellow DFLers were madder than hell at me for helping a Republican. I told them they could borrow a donkey—that didn't set well with them.

Yes, being Parks commissioner was fun. But over the years, something else started happening—and it wasn't good. The job was so demanding I was beginning to neglect my family.

When a politician gets elected, it's almost like his family gets elected too. I can see why so many politicians get divorced. I was so fortunate to have a dear and understanding woman for my wife such as Florence.

She enjoyed some parts of the political life. I took her to political parties, and we had Gov. and Mrs. Karl Rolvaag over one night for an Italian dinner soon after I was elected. They both were down-to-earth people and we enjoyed their company. (He gave me a quarter. Why, I don't remember. I still have it.)

We attended the little people's banquet together, too. It was one of the most delightful nights of my life. I was a guest of honor for about 100 people at the event, almost all of them 3 or 4 feet tall. The most well-known person there was actor Billy

Barty, who made dozens of movies. Florence and I had a wonderful time.

But I also asked her to represent me officially at some social gatherings that were political in nature. And sometimes, about once or twice a year, I had her represent me at tough meetings with constituents, meetings where I knew I wouldn't win regardless of the outcome. She always did an admirable job.

The 1970 campaign for my third term was difficult. Most every night after meetings at playgrounds, churches, even homes, John Ricci and I would go to bars. My favorite club was a piano bar at Mr. Joe's. There I met Bruno Leone, an excellent piano artist who later played in my band before he became CEO of Greenhaven Press, a successful publishing company.

Everyone loved me at Mr. Joe's. I finally figured out why—I bought a lot of drinks for the patrons. I was getting a reputation of drinking too much, and a reputation of not working as hard as I should, though I never neglected my duties. A lot of my supporters were disappointed in me, and they chose not to help me.

Doug Kelm, a powerful DFL leader, convinced his allies at the nominating convention not to endorse me for my re-election. But he had them abstain only. I respected him for that because had they voted against me, I wouldn't have been endorsed. That would have been disastrous for me on Election Day. As Chris Nicosia, a Republican councilmember said, in Ramsey County, you could be a gorilla and with DFL endorsement you'd still get elected.

Yes, in 1970 I was Mr. Ego, but I wised up. I quit the nightclub scene and won my third term. All my campaigns after the third one were successful. In all, I ran 11 times, five times without an opponent.

For quite some time it was said Tedesco couldn't be beat—except by his wife, Florence.

CHAPTER 60

The Mayor Makes a Speech in Italian

In 1971, Florence and I went on a tour of Italy. We spent quite a bit of time in Rome. Being a Catholic, I had the Vatican on my must-see list. We had an audience with Pope Paul VI, along with several hundred other people, and I visited the catacombs. We also went to Florence, Naples and Turin, and made a side trip to the village of my parents, Cotronei.

Angelo Pariana, a third or fourth cousin of mine, was the mayor of Cotronei. He came to St. Paul about 1974 to see the Pariana family, who were also his cousins.

I took him to City Hall and introduced him to the City Council during a meeting in the chambers. I'll never forget what happened next. He began to address the council—in Italian. He must have thought we were all indigenous Italian.

CHAPTER 61

Sleepover at City Hall

I WAS VERY UNPOPULAR WITH my fellow commissioners when I fought the "pay raise" for City Council members in July 1971.

It wasn't that the council didn't deserve a pay raise. It was the idea of Mayor Charlie McCarty trying to ram it down everyone's throats, which was his style.

"Supermayor" Charlie McCarty was brilliant, but he was always looking for a fight. Rosalie Butler, another DFL council member, helped him out quite a bit in that department. He sure made me mad in May, just a few months before the pay raise vote, when he tried to trick me into going to a conference about cities in Indianapolis on a day when he said nothing important was coming before the council. In fact, two important matters were to be voted on that day: a solid-waste ordinance and a proposed reduction in city sewer rates. If I hadn't stopped by my office on the way to the airport, I wouldn't have seen the agenda with those two items on it.

I stayed for the meeting and helped get both items passed.

McCarty had wanted to delay the sewer-rate reduction, but with me at the meeting, the DFL majority was united.

In the pay-raise matter, McCarty was insisting on an annual raise of almost $20,000 for himself, from $15,200 to $35,000—a raise of well over 100 percent—and a big increase for the council, too: $9,000, to take them from $14,000 to $23,000 a year.

I tried to offer an amendment that would provide a lesser pay raise to take effect after the next election. I figured that we knew what our salary was when we ran for office, and we shouldn't raise our own pay. Under my amendment, the mayor's salary would rise to only $28,500, and council salaries to $18,500. McCarty grabbed the paper with the amendment out of the council clerk's hands and walked out of the chamber after adjourning the session on his own—not legal, in the opinion of the city lawyers.

I was so mad I told McCarty I wouldn't leave the council chambers until he agreed to let the council hear my amendment. With the meeting adjourned, everyone drifted out of the room. I called my deputy, John Ricci, to bring me some papers and I settled in to work. Several people brought me food, and Florence brought me supper.

I stayed overnight, sleeping in the press room, which adjoins the council chambers. Several times during the night the phone rang and when I answered it, the callers would start yelling. "Tedesco, what the hell are you trying to do, show off?" I think it was angry DFLers, insiders of the party.

I ended my sleep-in the next day. We had the vote the next morning—it was 6 to 1, mine being the only "no" vote.

The council members were really angry at me. I ran into so much guff, but conveniently, we had already booked a trip to Martinique, so I got out of town. A week or so later, when I returned, the council had voted to rescind the raise. They got a lot of heat from noisy constituents who kept showing up at council meetings.

The council eventually followed my suggestion in a smaller way—a cost of living increase each year tied to a certain mid-level professional position. If they had taken my advice in the first place, they would have gotten more in their paychecks over the years.

CHAPTER 62

Champs of the Chamber

I SERVED WITH 27 COUNCIL MEMBERS in my 11 terms. All were dedicated, most were well-qualified, and several were not fit for the job. They were good guys, but they just didn't have "it."

Of the 27, I put myself at about eighth- to tenth-best in government service. In terms of public relations and people skills I put myself absolute first. I worked hard at pleasing the public. My approach to political problems was to look at them from the "man in the street" point of view—I'd had practice with that point of view back at WSHB in 1949 and on WCOW from 1950 to 1951 when I did man-on-the-street interviews.

Rosalie Butler was extremely qualified. Rosalie, along with her husband, was big in DFL politics. They were big supporters of candidates and the party. She was one tough lady who was always butting heads with McCarty. She was an extremely hard worker, but sometimes misunderstood. Just as some of our DFL friends thought I was showboating, so did they feel that way about Rosalie. Rosalie was news, she made contentious comments most of the time, but not once did I doubt her sincerity.

She didn't particularly like me at first. But she learned that I liked my job, did it well and made it look easy, and was a hard worker, on top of issues. She served from 1970 to 1979 and died in office.

Another excellent council person, who served from 1974 to 1977, was Bob Sylvester, who eventually became Susan Kimberly through a sex-change operation. She was extremely bright, in my opinion the smartest person to serve on the City Council. She went on to hold positions of importance with U.S. Sen. Norm Coleman and Saint Paul Mayor Randy Kelly.

Bob Sprafka, who served from 1968 to 1973, did the area a big service. He was an insurance agent in his "day job" and he put his talents to work as a Metropolitan Airports commissioner (in addition to our council positions, we served on other commissions). He discovered that the insurance premiums at the airport were excessive and saved the commission $100,000 in one year by getting the policies reworked. At that time his City Council pay was $12,000. Nice work, Robert.

I would have to name Bob Peterson as the number one council person during my tenure. He knew the city, had his facts straight and a straightforward delivery, and you just knew he knew what he was talking about. He served more than two decades, from 1944 to 1970, and went out as a defeated candidate.

CHAPTER 63

The Changing Charter

But a big change in the city charter had taken effect in June 1972 when council members elected in April were sworn in. No longer heads of departments, we were legislators only. Ruby Hunt, elected to the council for the first time that year, had been instrumental in getting the charter changed.

Under the commissioner system, all council members were elected at large. Now we would still be elected at-large, with a seventh council member added, but no longer would council members be commissioners of city departments. We would be legislators only. The mayor would be administrative head of the city and responsible for drawing up budgets, but wouldn't take part in council deliberations.

Two years later, another twist was added. The "alley system" was put in place, and at-large elections were over. Each candidate had to apply for a certain seat, meaning candidates could choose to run directly against a particular council member.

I felt the old commission-type government was the best the city ever had. The commissioner heading a department was directly responsible to the public. In my opinion, the at-large system wasn't as responsible—none of us was the head of a department, so each of us was only one-seventh to blame for anything that went wrong. And the mayor's position was "strong mayor." He had final say in all matters.

Finally in the 1980s Saint Paul went to the ward system, and I became the only City Council person in the city's history to serve in all three forms of government. I think the ward system was the worst. All you had to concern yourself with was looking out for your own ward. And don't let any council members tell you their primary concern isn't their own backyard.

CHAPTER 64

Invaluable in the Office

W HEN THE COUNCIL MEMBERS had to give up being commissioners of departments, the talk was that we no longer would
have deputies. For six years John Ricci had been my very able
assistant, and we both were concerned about what was to become of him. All went well, he passed a civil service test and
stayed with Parks and Rec. I always thought John was a loyal,
dedicated guy and friend. Now, so many years later, I think of
him in that regard even more so.

In my 21 years in office, I had four deputies or aides or as-
sistants, call them what you want. Ricci, my first deputy, was a
perfect fit for the job with street smarts that helped me become
a high-profile council member.

It was his idea to have his brother Bill's Army truck in our
campaign parades. This was no ordinary truck—it was vintage
World War I, with wheels riding on hard rubber tires. It caught
the eye of parade goers and got us a lot of attention for doing
the unusual. Eventually, Bill Ricci donated the truck to the
Smithsonian Institution in Washington, D.C.

John and I were a great team. I was the front man and he
handled the details, like the complaint he got from a constituent
one night at midnight.

Rather than giving the guy hell for calling him at an ungodly
hour, John went ahead and took care of the matter and called the
guy back to let him know the results—round about midnight.
The constituent, madder than hell, said to John, "What the hell

you doing calling me at midnight?" John replied, "That's when you called me." Enough said.

Marilyn Lantry, who later became a state senator, was my second deputy, only the powers that be had decided they would be called aides now that there were no commissioners to be deputies to. She had strong labor ties, which helped me tremendously. The labor leadership was no different from any other support group. There were good guys and bad guys, and Marilyn had the ability to juggle them around to our way of thinking.

Then there was Mike Sirian, a lifelong friend who had also worked for me at WCOW. Mike was a bookworm who knew government inside and out and helped establish compost locations around the city. He was a tremendous asset to me, but chose to return to the city clerk's office after a few months to protect his civil service status. Lastly I had Sue Vanelli. She was a doll—well-liked by the 17 neighborhood councils. Her attendance at neighborhood functions was rewarding to my office. All four deputies fit the bill, seemed made to order for whatever city government was in force at the time.

I don't count as one of my aides the woman who served for a couple of hours.

Once the dust had settled over the title to be carried by the people who would assist the council members after the 1972 charter change, I hired as my assistant Mae Benshoof, a political veteran who knew the way around City Hall. As the political season started for the spring 1972 election, John and Mae and I got together in my office to tell Mae the rudiments of the job. All went well until she said, "Of course, you know I'm going to help Charlie McCarty at re-election time." John and I were stunned. One of the paramount duties of an aide is to direct and manage the campaign to get her boss re-elected.

By mutual agreement, she quit. She probably had the shortest tenure of any employee in the city's history. I don't think she got paid.

McCarty didn't have many friends in City Hall or in the city at this time. He had been butting heads with the council for two years. Also, his early spat with Sister Giovanni didn't help his reputation.

Sister Giovanni was one of the most respected people in the city of Saint Paul, and she was a driving force behind the Guadalupe Area Project, which served the Hispanic community on the West Side. The Guadalupe project wanted to build a co-operative housing development on the former site of a church, preserving the church's tower. The project was to be called Torre de San Miguel, honoring that church. But the city wanted to tear down the tower, or "torre." Sister Giovanni came before the council in 1970 in her full black-and-white habit and protested, and Charlie yelled at her.

"You're in my ballpark now, Sister, and I'll tell you how it's going to be," he declared.

Councilman Len Levine came to the good sister's defense.

"This is the people's park, not yours, Mayor McCarty," he said.

I couldn't believe Charlie was so stupid as to get in a pissing contest with the West Side's most respected and loved person. I think that was the beginning of the end of his political career.

But he committed the biggest sin of all in politics, in my opinion, when he "forgot the girl that brought him to the dance"—political supporters such as Jerry Issacs, Harold Speak, even me. Charlie became the only incumbent mayor in the history of Saint Paul to be defeated in the primary election while running for re-election.

CHAPTER 65

Finding the Two-Faced Guy

ONE BAD THING ABOUT CITY POLITICS: Every two years you had to run for re-election.

You always had problems with opposing candidates trying to unseat you, but the real problem was so-called supporters stabbing you in the back.

One year we sent out self-addressed, stamped envelopes to our friends for financial support, as usual. We got several envelopes back, not only without financial donations, but with enclosures of nasty letters degrading me. Of course, the letters were unsigned. But I knew how to find out who the individual was.

We sent out another round of stamped, self-addressed envelopes asking for campaign donations. We wrote numbers hidden under the stamp of the envelope to be returned and kept track of who got the numbers. Number 1 was to Jones, 2 to Smith, etc.

Sure enough, back came a nasty letter. We checked the number under the envelope's stamp. It was from a guy with a good position in City Hall. Whenever he saw me he would shower me with kind words. How he could be so two-faced? He gave meaning to the old saying, "Don't worry about your enemies, it's your friends you have to look out for."

But mostly the campaigns had their fun times as the candidates crossed paths. Republican George Vavoulis and I got to know each other on my first campaign, back in 1966, when he was running for re-election as mayor (Tom Byrne defeated him). I liked him; he was a respected businessman.

He noticed I was a hardworking candidate. We ran across

each other almost every morning at plant gates. And I was always there before him—he mentioned this many times after the
campaign. One day several years later, he came to see me about
a problem his church, Saint George's Greek Orthodox Church,
was having with the city of Saint Paul. There was some neighborhood opposition to the church's plan to expand at its location on Summit Avenue, one of the tonier streets in the city. The
variance needed was five feet. I was happy to grant it. Despite
Vavoulis being a Republican, he became a strong supporter of
mine.

Many years later, in 2005, I ran across his widow, Beverly,
when she had a booth in the skyway in downtown Saint Paul
for an arts and crafts event for which my band was playing. She
reminded me how grateful for my help the parishioners of her
church still were.

On another occasion, David Hozza was outside the Civic
Center on a cold night shaking hands with hockey fans arriving
for a game of the Saint Paul Fighting Saints of the now-defunct
World Hockey Association. Meanwhile, I was inside at center
ice singing the national anthem before 12,000 of them. Hozza
was heard to ask, in some kind of friendly manner, "How does
Tedesco do it?"

CHAPTER 66

The Frosting on the Landmark Cake

THE 1972 ELECTION WAS MY FOURTH. Because of the charter change, my wonderful six years as Parks and Rec commissioner were over. But I was approaching one of the most important actions I would take in my 21 years in office, though I didn't realize it at the time.

DFLer Larry Cohen had been elected mayor, and with the addition of the seventh council member on the ballot, the DFLers won a majority of the seats with four. Since the mayor was no longer on the council, he had to approach allies in the chamber to get his bills proposed.

One day Frank Marzitelli came to my office. He had been on the City Council years earlier, but now was chief administrator for the city. He said he was representing Mayor Cohen, and that Cohen wanted to tear down the old Federal Courts Building.

Frank was an operator who liked to go with the flow. He tended to side with anybody he thought would prevail in any political dispute. He was even on record publicly as supporting the rescue, which had started as far back as 1967, when Mayor Tom Byrne tried to get the ball rolling. That first effort didn't take off, but in 1969, Byrne appointed a mayor's committee, and from then until 1972 it was one thing after another that citizens and politicians overcame to make the deal work.

Neither Charlie McCarty, Byrne's successor, nor Larry Cohen,

McCarty's successor, was on the record publicly as opposing the rescue of the building.

Still, Frank was Cohen's right-hand man as the city administrator, so I had to take seriously his pronouncement that Cohen wanted it down, even though I had heard no direct comment from Cohen.

The situation in 1972 stood like this: The federal government was willing to sell its surplus building if the city of Saint Paul would agree to pay for heating and upkeep.

When Frank came to me, he was howling and cussing. Did I know how much it was going to cost the city to heat that [expletive] building? he asked. It was only good, he said, for making riprap (broken chunks of stone that help prevent riverbank erosion).

I was familiar with the old building because of my custom of entertaining senior citizens at various locations throughout the city, including the Wilder Center, a community center funded by the Amherst H. Wilder Foundation. The center stood across Rice Park from the old Federal Courts.

Frank said that once the structure was gone, the city would keep the location as open green space to complement Rice Park.

The courts building, opened in 1902, was run down and had been closed for several years. But it was still a stately, beautiful building in need of a little loving tender care. Its location on Rice Park showed promise. On the east side of the park was the Saint Paul Hotel, also somewhat rundown but still as elegant as when it opened in 1910. Directly across the park was the central branch of the Saint Paul Public Library, finished in 1917 in an Italian-Renaissance-revival style. The Wilder Center, built in 1913, was on the fourth side.

I wasn't impressed with the Federal Courts demolition plan. I had been to Europe, where they were saving old buildings, not destroying them. I was one of the City Council members who had been named to the board of Minnesota Landmarks, the nonprofit group that was engineering the rescue, and I became determined to save the old Federal Courts.

There hadn't been a lot of talk among City Council members about saving the old building until I started lobbying them. It wasn't a hard sell. We voted to have the city pay for heat and upkeep, the last element needed for the rescue. The city bought the building from the federal government for a dollar, then gave it to Ramsey County. The county paid for the restoration and turned the building over to a reorganized Minnesota Landmarks.

I had no idea the building would become the stately structure that opened in 1978. My only thought was to move senior-citizen activities from the Wilder Center to the first floor of the Federal Courts, and use the upper floors for quasi-governmental and arts offices—the Schubert Club, the Women's Institute, etc.

The Schubert Club does have its offices there, along with other arts and cultural organizations, and there are

Eugene McCarthy, at left, I and Miles Lord craned our necks to see the newly built Federal Courts Building on Robert Street in Saint Paul. The old Federal Courts Building became the Landmark Center.

performances in music, dance and theater, as well as exhibitions and public forums.

The Wilder Center made way in 1985 for the modern architectural style of the Ordway Center for Performing Arts, and across the park, the Saint Paul Hotel was refurbished in the early 1980s to join the Landmark Center, the Ordway and the library on the borders of Rice Park. I've traveled to 46 of the Lower 48 states, and very few parks in the country can compare with Rice Park and its setting of architectural gems.

Probably the biggest disappointment of my political career was that no one recognized my efforts to save the old Federal Courts. I was the most popular politician in Saint Paul at the time, and if I had gone along with Frank's demolition plan, the council would have gone along with Frank, and the building would have gone to the wrecking ball—and the work of many fine people would have gone to waste.

I'll go to my grave swearing that without me, that building was coming down!! Period!!

CHAPTER 67

The Tough Year

THE YEAR 1973 STARTED OFF well enough. The council was a lot calmer with McCarty out of office and a DFL majority on the council. But soon enough, things got tough. My papa died in January. He had been retired since 1959.

In 1968, the city had taken my parents' house in Little Italy by eminent domain for a highway that was never built. My dad thought he had struck it rich: He got $15,800 for a house he had bought in 1926 for $1,200, that was improved so much by my brother Nick's repairs. But when my dad went looking for another home, he could find nothing comparable to that one. My folks ended up renting, and for various reasons, they had to move three times in the last five years of my dad's life.

I think losing his house hastened his death.

At the funeral home, I placed a religious medal in the pocket of his suitcoat. All his children were at the services, and we buried Papa in the cold of winter.

A 1927 Irving Berlin song stuck with me for days: "The song is ended but the melody lingers on." I'll never forget my papa.

My mother went to live with her only surviving daughter, Mary, and Mary's husband, Alfred Gentile, for about two years until going to live in a nursing home. She died in 1978. I still have a tape of my mother singing, but I can't bring myself to listen to it. I just end up crying.

My brother-in-law, Al Gentile, was the closest thing you could find to a saint. A gentle, caring man, he received the Distinguished Flying Cross in the Pacific Theater during World

Father Thomas Pingatore offered a special blessing at Saint Ambrose
on the occasion of my parents' 50th wedding anniversary in 1962.

War II and never once bragged about it or mentioned it. In fact,
I loved my brother-in-law Al as much as I did my brothers Nick
and Albert.

In our early years we brothers had been very close. Nick was
the oldest, and sometimes would remind us of that. Albert was
three years younger than me. He and I played together and sold
newspapers together. All three of us got along well, and had
worked together for years in the radio-station business.

The year 1973 was also the year I made a comeback attempt
in that business. It was not a wise decision. I had been primarily
a public servant since 1966, and only secondarily in the radio
business. The old saying "you can't serve two masters" was right
on the money in my case.

And Nick wasn't with me this time. He and I spent more than
20 years together, week by week, running radio stations. He had
his shortcomings and I had mine, but we seemed to complement
each other's abilities, and I missed his help in this venture.

With several businessmen, I was the major stockholder of a group that purchased KCGO for $250,000 in Cheyenne, Wyo. We planned to upgrade the station by increasing its power from 500 watts to 10,000 watts, and we eventually did. But nothing went right, anything that could go wrong did, and we had four months of utter confusion before putting the station up for sale. Several buyers were interested, among them the movie star Darren McGavin. The least most likely to purchase the station was a dentist from Pennsylvania, and he did, for $190,000. I lost $75,000, and it took me five years to meet my obligations. Was I happy to finally rid myself of that lemon.

CHAPTER 68

The Shoe Leather Meets the Streets

I HAD BEEN IN NEVER-NEVER LAND my first six years on the council. I thought the prestige and fun of being commissioner of Parks and Rec would go on forever. Now I was merely a council member.

But there were still surprises to keep life interesting.

One evening I saw a TV news clip showing U.S. Sen. William Proxmire, D-Wis., working in a factory. Bingo, I say to myself, what a great idea. I announced I would spend one of my weeks of vacation each year doing city employees' jobs. I had my first chance at a week's work in July 1974.

On Monday, I went to work on the garbage truck. And I did work. I didn't want anyone to say I was loafing on the job.

Garbage hauler was one of the many city jobs I worked to show support for Saint Paul city workers.

Susan Spencer covered the event for WCCO-TV. It was her first assignment at the station; she went on to CBS in Washington, D.C. All the other TV stations covered the garbage-truck event as well. It really wasn't bad work, not as tough as Tuesday, that hot summer day when I worked with a street-patching crew spreading asphalt. I think my legs and back were hurting for days.

Wednesday I helped bathe an elephant at my old stomping ground, Como Zoo. In the rest of the week, I walked along with a water-meter reader and traveled with cops and firefighters.

My police job was to patrol in the Selby-Dale area with two black police officers, Corky Benner and Bill Finney. Finney later became the chief of the Saint Paul Police Department. Most of the day was boring. I still remember Bill Finney's words—"Hours of boredom, minutes of sheer fright. On one call." His words came true when we were called to an apartment complex on a domestic. A woman came running out of the building, screaming, and she was bleeding profusely. Her boyfriend had cut her up with a razor.

My firefighting day was spent at the fire house on Payne Avenue just up from Seventh Street. It was a little like the police experience—boring until we got a call. Then it became downright dangerous for the real fire fighters.

The fire was downtown in the Lowry Building. I was in full attire for the situation—helmet, boots, rubber coat with flannel lining. The firefighters didn't let me get near the fire while they were pouring water on it from their hoses. My job was to sweep away the water that was making the floors slippery.

Speaking of firemen, they are the most powerful political group in Saint Paul. The DFL, and I suppose the Republican Party, mostly give lip service to their candidates. But the firemen campaign door to door, in uniform, for or against you. You don't want to get them teed off. I had their support in nine of 11 elections. I guess a couple of times I did not support their causes. Apparently they weren't too angry with me as they didn't work too hard against me.

I must say they eat good, and if you're invited for lunch or dinner at a station house, don't pass it up.

Firefighting wasn't the only hot summertime job. Street repairmen had to work with steaming asphalt.

When I got back to council work, I suggested that the city find cooler summer wear for that job. Those flannel-lined rubber coats were awful in the heat.

I did about 40 different city jobs over the eight years that I took my "vacation work week." I operated an elevator at City Hall, and swept the sidewalks too. I worked as a librarian at the Sun Ray branch on Saint Paul's East Side.

And I spent a day with the health inspector. We went to a house on Stewart Street on the west end. The place was filthy. Dog dung all over the house—you had to walk in an aisle because there was so much debris. I just can't see how people can live like that. The tenants were given a citation to clean up the feces and the junk in a hurry. I actually went home ill. It was a short day for me.

I also did jobs that weren't on the city payroll, but were related to places that were licensed by the city, since I was chairman of that committee. In a nursing home, I gave baths to Alzheimer's patients who called me every name in the book, and I tended bar and drove a cab.

And I stayed overnight in the city morgue. The morgue had various-size jars sitting around with body parts in them. I understand they were kept as evidence in court cases. There were no calls while I was there, and about 4 A.M. I begged off and went home. What a boring job!

CHAPTER 69

Gay Rights and Responsibilities

In THE 1970s, POLITICS WERE CHANGING in Saint Paul. The DFL Party—and some of my constituents—was becoming more one-issue oriented: gay rights, anti-abortion, pro-life.

In July 1974, I was the only City Council member to vote against the gay-rights bill, which passed.

I feel differently now, especially about equal opportunity for employment: These days I don't care what race, nationality, sexual orientation or other circumstances are attached to a person who wants a job. If that person can lift the fire hose or explain algebra, I'm for that person getting the job as a firefighter or teacher. But I do think that a teacher needs to keep his or her sexual orientation private and not talk about it with students.

But in 1974, I voted against gay rights. My vote had some contradictions in it. Barb Metzer, a lesbian, wanted to become a firefighter. I supported her right to do that, but I opposed gay rights overall.

After the gay-rights vote, Barb brought me a rose.

I said, "Barb, why the rose? I did not vote for you."

She said, "We knew we didn't have your vote—you were the only one who was honest with us."

The rest of the council members buckled under the pressure of the gay-rights groups and supporters who packed the City Council chambers the day of the vote. Many times, we council members, me included, would have to take into consideration whether a packed chamber represented the views of the entire city. But we didn't think that those who attended the council meetings were more dedicated, for or against the matter in question.

Dennis Miller, another gay-rights activist, said he always voted for me because I was kind to his grandparents. I had entertained them and been respectful to them.

Old folks like a little attention—ask me, I'm one of them!

CHAPTER 70

The Door to Washington Swings Open

In 1976, Joe Karth, a well-respected congressman from the Fourth District, decided not to run for re-election. Dozens were hot to run for his seat. Bob Hess, his assistant, appeared to be the heir apparent.

Personally, I don't think Bob wanted the job. I toyed with it. A great number of people wanted me to run for Congress.

R. William Reilly, one of the brains behind all my campaigns, came up with a brilliant idea. Since I had no competition for my council seat in the primary election or the general election, we ran an eye-catching ad, professionally designed, at four columns wide and the full length of the newspaper page.

"Do you want to send me to Congress?" the ad said. "I don't have an opponent for my council seat. If you do, please vote for me [for the council]. It will indicate you do wish me to run for Congress."

Well, I ran first!! And by a healthy number of votes. Did the public want me to represent them in Congress or did they just want to get me off the City Council? I'm sure it was to represent them in Congress.

But I had a heart-to-heart talk with Florence. We had been in politics for 10 years at that point, and no way was she going to move to Washington. Although my children were not as adamant as my wife, they weren't too excited about moving either.

Me, alone in Washington, D.C. I just didn't know what I

would do without Florence and the family. I'm glad I decided not to run.

Our family supported DFLer Bruce Vento, a decent, bright young schoolteacher. In the 1976 election, voters picked him to succeed Karth. And George Latimer was elected to his first term as Saint Paul mayor, the fourth mayor I served.

CHAPTER 71

The Best Mayors

GEORGE LATIMER EVENTUALLY WON four terms, and he probably could have been reelected forever. He was handsome, a smooth attorney who could hobnob with the working people in the daytime and go to the Ordway at night in a tux. George was good for the city.

Larry Cohen, the first Jew to be mayor of Saint Paul, was underestimated, in my opinion. He had such an easy-going manner and made everything look easy.

But, as a retired City Council member, I would consider getting myself in trouble in order to say that the best mayor of all for accomplishments was Norm Coleman. In his two terms, he was instrumental in getting the city the Lawson Building and the new Minnesota Mutual Building and best of all, he brought a major-league sport back to St. Paul: the National Hockey League's Minnesota Wild, and a new arena to put them in. The Minnesota North Stars departed from the old Civic Center in 1993. You get in the new Xcel Center and it's hard to believe you're in Saint Paul.

And I have nothing but good things to say about Mayor Randy Kelly. I actively supported him in 2002, when Coleman stepped away from the city—and the Democratic Party—to run for the U.S. Senate, as a Republican.

CHAPTER 72

My Word Is My Vote

For most of my years on the City Council, at least once a month we voted for sidewalks in different sections of town. There were always a dozen or so people against new sidewalks, multiplied by 52 weeks became potentially 600 voters against new sidewalks. Councilpersons Leonard Levine and Rosalie Butler always voted against the sidewalks, making them instant heroes. My feeling was, if I have sidewalks in front of my house, why shouldn't you have them in front of yours? But enough of this nonsense—why should two labor-endorsed candidates keep vot-

Rosalie Butler was a strong-willed City Council member who learned to appreciate me as a hard worker. Behind us is Council member Len Levine.

ing against sidewalks, while the rest of us were the "bad guys" voting to spend money? So in 1971, I started to vote against new sidewalks.

All hell broke loose. The three of us had a little talking-to by union bosses, whose union members got the jobs when sidewalks were built. All of a sudden the votes were unanimous—we all wanted sidewalks.

I always tried to be "up front" in my voting. Only once I did not keep my word. I had given my word to George Latimer I would support a certain candidate for the planning board. Subsequently I learned that if he got the job, he would be "triple-dipping" in government funds through pensions and other stipends. I changed my mind and voted no. Principle was involved here. George probably felt the same, as he removed me from the Metropolitan Airports Commission, the best committee I served on.

Maybe I liked MAC because there was always something of interest going on at the airport: expansion of gates, runways, vendor contracts and so on. It also didn't hurt that we got $100 for each monthly meeting and we got a national and an international trip each year. I went to London and Ireland with Florence, and with son Tony to Hawaii, Mexico, Los Angeles, San Francisco and New York.

But when I crossed George over the potential triple-dipper, he took me off MAC. I was hurt and bitter, but time heals all wounds. I later played for one of his re-election parties gratis.

CHAPTER 73

Busted!

As chairman of the license committee, I supposedly was a powerful person. That didn't keep me from being busted in August 1977 when I went undercover as a license inspector during my vacation work week.

During the day, I spent time behind a City Hall counter issuing licenses, and then went into the field checking picnic licenses. But at night, I went undercover—I took off my wig.

With real license inspectors, I went to check out an "all-night tippling house" that sold booze well after the closing time specified in city ordinances for licensed taverns and bars. When the police came, they arrested me, a well-known public figure, because no one knew what I looked like without my wig. They let me go.

CHAPTER 74

Even Caught on Tape!

Being the license-committee chairman meant an automatic campaign donation from almost every bar owner in town. Joe Carchedi, a cop on leave, was the license inspector. He was a brazen, no-nonsense, tough individual. A lot of people didn't like him. They thought he took bribes, just as people think all us politicians do. However, I never detected any wrongdoing of my colleagues on any level, in my 21 years of service.

Perhaps Joe didn't pay for many meals on the job. Maybe he was in a club at lunch or dinnertime and the owner invited him to have a bite to eat. Someone put a complaint to the state because they began an investigation, not only of Carchedi, but also me!!

The state sent two undercover cops and a nightclub owner, Bill Heinie, to my office. They said they wanted to talk about moving another liquor license to Randolph Avenue near Snelling Avenue.

Many businessmen came before the City Council with high-priced lawyers, seeking transfers of one kind or another. More often than not, they didn't need a lawyer along.

In this case, the second license would be near Joe LaNasa's Bar. They asked me how I felt about that.

I remember saying something like—hey, the neighbors don't squawk, it's OK with me. Heinie insisted I take $200. I said no, but he insisted, so finally I took it. But much to their dismay, as we walked out of my inner office, I called out to my assistant, Marilyn Lantry.

"Marilyn, give a hundred of this money to [Dave] Hozza's campaign committee, he's not doing too well. And be sure to deposit this $100 in our campaign committee."

Unbeknownst to me, the police were in the Radisson Garage across the street from my office, using electronic equipment to tape the conversation on audiocassettes.

Checks or cash donations to campaign committees, properly disclosed, are legal. Take money the way those guys were offering it, and I would have been in hot water. Many times over the years people offered me money. I would turn them down and say, you can help me at campaign time. Most of the time they didn't.

Mayor Latimer called me down to his office to discuss the tape of the meeting. You do have some rough language, he said to me. I had used the "F" word several times and some slang. It wasn't exactly material for prime-time TV.

George asked me if I wanted to make the conversation public. I said, hell, yes!! If the contents didn't come out that day, they would tomorrow, the next week or the next month.

We had a big news conference in the mayor's office in time for the 6 o'clock TV news and the morning editions of the newspapers. Not much to report—an honest politician. Wow!!

CHAPTER 75

The Cable Controversy

In 1978, I was the top vote-getter in the primary. (On Election Day, I ran first in five of 11 elections.) In June, at Latimer's second inauguration, I predicted on stage that George would go into the history books as one of the finest mayors St. Paul would ever have. But his 1983 veto of the council's decision about cable companies, in my second year as chairman of the council, still rankles.

In the 1970s, the Federal Communications Commission had ruled that cable TV had to be accessible to members of the public who wanted to air programs. Saint Paul council members had

been looking at cable operations throughout the United States before deciding which company to choose to provide service to the city.

On one fact-finding trip, I was able to determine that fewer than 100 people were watching a particular cable channel in Columbus, Ohio. But that was the beauty of cable TV—it was designed with many channels to satisfy most viewers' needs. We visited Reading, Pa.—I thought a very depressed area. The only thing I remember about Reading is that the guy hawking cars on a Philadelphia TV station for a local dealer was the same guy who has been doing spots forever for Tousley Ford in the Twin Cities.

We went to a cable TV convention in San Francisco, stayed at the Mark Hopkins Hotel. When I found out it was $105 a night, I was upset and came home early. Even though it wasn't my money, I treated it as though it was.

In San Antonio, Tex., Council Member Jim Scheibel stayed at the best hotel; I stayed at the Travelodge. In Atlanta, Mayor Charlie McCarty had a suite; I stayed at a small hotel across the street. Guess growing up in Little Italy made you happy staying at moderately priced hotels and motels.

The time to vote came in July 1983. I first voted for Nor-West Cable Communications Partnership, a local group of prominent business people, with women and minorities represented. Nor-West got the nod for the licenses on a 4 to 3 vote.

Mayor Latimer vetoed us, stating the local group didn't pass the "smell test." He was concerned that they lacked experience working on cable as a team, and that they were underfunded.

I think the words "smell test" were extreme. Nor-West, in my opinion, could have hired professionals with expertise to operate the system.

The council had entertained the idea of having the city operate the cable system, which I think could have been done. The only time the private companies joined forces was for a smear campaign about how inept the city would be if it elected to operate the system.

In any event none of the three council members allied with the mayor were going to change their votes. So I, as council president, realized we weren't going to be able to override George's veto and we ended up choosing Continental Cablevision of Boston, even though I thought we should have gone with local people who would spend money locally. Continental ran the station for several years, sold out, made millions and took the money to Boston.

CHAPTER 76

The Music Was Always Playing

THROUGHOUT MY COUNCIL CAREER, I kept playing music and singing whenever I had the chance, most often at nursing homes, senior citizens' homes and hospitals.

I sang the national anthem or "God Bless America" before at least 20 professional fight cards, thanks to my dear friend Jim O'Hara, boxing commissioner for the state of Minnesota. I had known him since I was a teenager. In fact, when I was 15 I had a crush on his wife-to-be, Kay.

Sometimes there were several hundred people in the audience and sometimes many thousands. One of the fights, featuring Scott LeDoux, was televised nationally on CBS. Yes, I sang the national anthem coast-to-coast on March 9, 1980.

Sitting in the front row at the Civic Center was Robert Goulet, popular actor and singer, who was appearing locally in "Camelot." He was a very nice, down-to-earth gentleman and I got to spend quite a bit of time with him.

I took the big band (17 musicians) out often as well. Once it was for a seniors' Christmas Party at the World Theater, sponsored by the Knights of Columbus of Roseville. Another time it was to play for the grand reopening of the Orpheum Theater in Saint Paul in 1979. The only theater in downtown Saint Paul at the time, it had been closed for years. The original Coney Island sandwich shop that I used to visit when I worked as a shoeshine boy was still around the corner on Saint Peter Street. The original owners' daughter, Mary Ellen Arvanitis, worked for me at City Hall from 1980 to 1987. The President, the theater where

my brother Nick and I worked, had been demolished years earlier to make way for the Commercial Bank, which in turn was
demolished to make way for a parking lot.

After the Orpheum's big opening, I arranged a Christmas program there for senior citizens. I paid $75 to rent the movie "Top
Hat" with Ginger Rogers and Fred Astaire. We had a full house.

The Orpheum closed again a year after the reopening. I hope
my singing didn't lead to its demise.

My band also played more than 30 Halloween parties at Gillette
Children's Hospital plus Christmas parties, many of them gratis,
and some sponsored by UNICO, an Italian-American group that
gives college scholarships to high school students who are of
Italian descent.

After the 1976 earthquake in the Udine area of Italy, I led a
16-piece band at the Prom in an event that raised $45,000 for
quake relief.

I also did a lot of entertaining for the Saint Paul Association
for Retarded Children, as well as being an active board member.

The re-opened Orpheum Theater
in downtown Saint Paul was the
site of one of my Christmas parties
for seniors.

It was cold work being a
Christmastime bell ringer for
the Salvation Army.

I was given an award in 1978 for my work with SPARC, and according to my dear friend Phyllis Soder, to that time I was the only elected politician to get such an honor.

My involvement with the Minnesota Youth Symphony was short-lived. In the early 1980s I was approached to sing a solo with them. At first I thought the director was kidding. He was not. My tenor solo went pretty well, I thought, for the program that was broadcast on KUOM-FM from Irondale Senior High School in New Brighton. But as quickly as the symphony entered my life, it left.

I enjoyed bringing Broadway to Minnesota by producing musicals for the St. Paul Opera Workshop, from "Showboat" to "Oklahoma" to "The Sound of Music." My main forte was raising the money for the shows; I left the directing to Max Metzger. I also sang with his band at his Sunday shows at Como Park.

And occasionally I reverted to my wild Western radio style. In the mid 1980s, I became Tex Tedesco for an all-night country-Western fund-raiser held at Mangini's Restaurant and broadcast on KTCR. We raised almost $4,000 that night for the Saint Paul Police Band.

A 1980s radio fund-raiser where I played "Tex Tedesco" brought back memories of being "Valley City Vic" in the early 1950s on radio station WCOW in South Saint Paul.

CHAPTER 77

Real Estate

I WAS IN THE REAL ESTATE BUSINESS for about five years with three partners in the 1970s. My partners—Pat Monno, the late Willie Olmer and the late Joe Lombardo, who had been an early political supporter of mine—had vast real estate backgrounds; I was the only novice in the group. We primarily bought and sold apartment buildings. Willie and Pat ran the business, collected the rents, handled the rentals, did all the repairs. Joe and I were investors. It worked quite well for a while, but the rental market soured, and Willie and Pat bought out Joe and I. I made a modest profit, better than a loss, as with some of my businesses.

Florence and I owned a small apartment building for a short time in the 1970s. She managed the units, kept the books, collected the rents. Sometimes tenants were unreasonable, sometimes dishonest.

One young woman was a great tenant until a young stud moved in with her. They tried to skip without paying the rent. Florence followed them to their new location, got the address, notified conciliation court and collected the rent. You have to get up early in the morning to get ahead of Florence—even then I don't think you could.

We got out of the rental business, and it was nice not to have any responsibilities, especially for Florence, who did all of the work.

CHAPTER 78

Nice Folks—Hollywood

I MET SO MANY CELEBRITIES in 21 years. I've forgotten many, but one person I'll never forget was Mary Tyler Moore. In the early 1970s, WCCO-TV had a press party for "The Mary Tyler Moore Show" in Minneapolis and there must have been a mix-up because my son, Tony, and I were the only ones at the party from Saint Paul. Tony and I had pictures taken with Mary Tyler Moore and her co-star, Valerie Harper. We actually spent quite a bit of time with them and they were especially nice to Tony, a teenager at the time. They even gave us their agent's address in Hollywood, and we did correspond with them for a short period.

Festivities surrounding the Saint Patrick's Day parade, which I helped start about 1967, gave me the opportunity to meet many movie stars, e.g., Eddie Albert, Julie London, and Forrest Tucker. I had met Pat O'Brien at the Saint Paul railroad depot in 1942 for a war-bond drive, and got to see him again about 40 years later when he came back for events pertaining to the Saint Patrick's Day parade. I spent a good amount of time with him and he was a friendly, amiable, all-around good guy.

CHAPTER 79

Big Wheels—Politics

I KNEW MANY POLITICIANS—Hubert Humphrey, Walter Mondale, Miles Lord and Eugene McCarthy. Gene McCarthy was not too popular with DFLers for a time. Many, many people felt his anti-war campaign as he sought the presidency in 1968 cost Hubert Humphrey, the eventual Democratic nominee, the presidency against Richard Nixon.

I like all the politicians I've known, but if I had to pick a favorite, it would be Walter Mondale, the former vice president and ambassador. He was a swell guy, and he didn't forget you. I was at a seminar at the Radisson Hotel in Saint Paul in about 2003 where he was the main speaker. After his talk, he came over to me and Florence and gave us a warm greeting. I'll bet everyone in the audience thought we were someone special.

Hubert Humphrey wrote me a beautiful personal note in 1973 when my father died. Here we posed with Duluth entrepreneur Geno Paulucci in the early 1970s.

I supported Mondale throughout his political career, including his bid for the U.S. Senate in 2002 when incumbent DFLer Paul Wellstone died in a plane crash less than two weeks before the election.

On Oct. 25, 2002, I was sitting in the dining room of the Treasure Island Casino in Red Wing, Minn., having lunch. My wife, Florence, and two of our friends, Irene Speak and Mike Majack, were playing the slots. A news flash showed up on TV: Sen. Wellstone had been killed in an airplane crash in northern Minnesota along with his wife, Sheila, his daughter, Marcia Wellstone Markuson, three staff members and two pilots.

Along with everyone else in the room, I was shocked. I first met the senator when I had to make a speech against him in 1982 at a DFL convention in Duluth. I was speaking on behalf of Bill Farmer, who was running for state auditor, as was Wellstone. Neither got elected.

Wellstone came off as pretty windy, but his style caught on as he became a well-liked and respected U.S. senator. With him gone, Coleman won the 2002 Senate race against Mondale. I hadn't been too happy with Wellstone, but I would have voted for him.

I had my picture taken with Ted Kennedy twice, before and after he became a senator. The second time around, he had a picture taken with my grandson, Justin Bloyer, when Justin was

Ted Kennedy and I were photgraphed during one of his earliest runs for the U.S. Senate.

less than a year old. Someone was going to send me the picture, but didn't. Ted Kennedy was not my cup of tea. I found him stuffy and arrogant. I'd still like to have that picture.

The nicest politician I met was Rudy Perpich, governor of the state of Minnesota—a gentleman, a man of his word—just a great guy. And a helluva polka dancer. Just ask my sister, Mary Gentile, she will tell you, "I danced the polka with the governor, Rudy Perpich."

I met John F. Kennedy just before his election as president in 1960, at the Minnesota Hippodrome. My band played for him gratis. I also led a five-piece band that played for Mike Dukakis when he ran for president in 1988. Dukakis was one of the nicest politicos I've met, maybe because he was the only one who paid the band for its services.

CHAPTER 80

National and International

As a councilman, I was able on more than one occasion to meet visiting dignitaries who arrived from foreign countries. I had the pleasure of spending an afternoon at a palatial residence on Summit Avenue when a Swedish ambassador was being entertained. At other times I met officials from Croatia and Sarajevo, and from Poland, when Poland was still a Communist country. My friends at the Polish-American Club in Saint Paul criticized me for meeting with a Communist, but in retrospect, I had to do it as part of my job of representing the city.

On the national level, I had opportunities to meet many black leaders at political conventions. Andrew Young, the well-respected civil rights leader and former mayor of Atlanta, I met in Houston. I met with the Rev. Jesse Jackson and supported him when he ran for president.

When Jackson came to a rally at Dale Street and University Avenue in Saint Paul, I participated. I had no problem mingling with blacks—I grew up with them.

One of the most delightful nights of my political career was a party in Atlanta with Bill Wilson, my friend and fellow council member with whom I shared a room on more than one council-related trip. The party went on all night, with me being the only white person among 25 to 30 blacks.

Before I met Jimmy Carter, I was in his inaugural parade in January 1977, riding on the float for the city of Saint Paul. I flew to Washington and, being on a tight budget, I stayed overnight at the home of some dedicated Democrats.

The float was to represent different ethnic groups living in Saint Paul, so the next day I donned an authentic Italian costume I had borrowed from Micholena and Russell Frascone. Micholena was an advocate of Italian-American causes in Saint Paul. I had a white shirt and black pants, red cape and black hat. I looked like a peasant. Henry Greencrow, an American Indian, was in his native attire. We also had Mexican, Scandinavian and other nationalities represented on the float.

It was no picnic. It was cold that day. Luckily I had put on long johns before I put on the peasant outfit.

I met President Carter later, on one of his visits to Saint Paul. We were in a procession line at the Landmark Center. As Carter came to shake my hand, I put my hand in my pocket to give him an invitation to my fund-raiser that night. Man, before you know, we were surrounded by his Secret Service men. I caused a lot of commotion at that event.

That day I also got to meet Leslie Stahl, a newswoman from CBS-TV. She looks much better now than she did then.

CHAPTER 81

An Advanced (in Age) Degree

On a couple of occasions I inquired about jobs in city government in Saint Paul and Minneapolis. I ran into a stumbling block—"college degree necessary." So I decided to get one.

I enrolled at Metropolitan State University about 1976. What a great institution. It took a practical approach—50 percent of your requirements for a degree was for life achievement. I got credit for being a general manager of radio stations, music, newspaper publishing, etc. It took me two years of attendance part-time at their downtown Saint Paul campus to earn the remaining credits.

I graduated in 1978 at the age of 55, the second-oldest person in the class. Metro State now has beautiful new buildings just east of downtown. What a treasure for the immediate East Side and downtown area. I am still a supporter of Metropolitan State and participate in their fund-raising activities and help promote their causes. Now they have a new library building that is a real treasure to the university and the neighborhood.

CHAPTER 82

On the Street Named for Me

One of the biggest days of my life was July 1, 1981, when I had a street named after me. Up until recently I was the only living person in Saint Paul with a street named after him.

Street naming kind of runs in the family. About 1960, radio station WISK, later KDWB, was located on the busiest street in Woodbury, then an unincorporated village. My brother Nick was asked to name it, and he did: Radio Drive. He also named the less-busy Tower Drive.

When I was on the City Council, I was able to name streets after my parents: Aïda Place in front of the Como Park Conservatory for my mother, and for my father, Antonio Drive, adjoining Highland Park Golf Course.

The plan about my street name was a secret for nearly a year as neighborhood activist Eileen Weida, my wife, Florence, and my deputy at the time, Susan Vanelli, worked on it. They worked with the City Council to make Collins Street, the three-block-long street where I grew up, into Tedesco Street.

Matt Morelli, owner of Morelli's Italian Market, was all for it even though it cost him to have all his stationery changed because his address was changing. Several residents complained they would have to buy new address labels. The three ladies bought them new address labels.

The council took action on the renaming while I was out of the chambers. The newspapers even got in on the act, agreeing not to publish the name change. I didn't find out until about a week before the date.

The day a Saint Paul street was named for me, July 1, 1981, was one of the biggest days of my life. My son, Tony, did the honors in removing the covering to reveal the sign.

The ladies did a magnificent job of putting the program together. We had coffee and soft drinks and doughnuts for the public at the Labor Plaza, 500 Tedesco St. The plaza is exactly where my folks' home stood. It was the only house my immigrant mom and dad owned in America.

We then gathered at Payne Avenue and Tedesco Street in front of Morelli's store. The police band was there, along with a crowd of about 300 people. Matt Morelli was the master of ceremonies.

I had made arrangements with Bloomberg Electronics to videotape the whole program for my personal use. To my dismay, we had picture, but no sound. But the Lord must have been looking out for me that day because KMSP, Channel 9, taped the event in its entirety, with picture and sound, and gave it to me as a gift.

Mayor George Latimer was principal speaker. He did an excellent job—interspersing a few key Italian words. I think George is of Lebanese and Italian descent. Then I gave a speech recognizing Father Thomas Pingatore; my brother Nick and his wife, Helen; my brother Al and his wife-to-be, Linda Frenrich; my sister, Mary Gentile, and her husband, Alfred Gentile. I then recognized my son, Tony, who later became an assistant city attorney for Saint Paul—how proud I was of him—and my two daughters, Patricia Ann, a medical technician, and Elizabeth Louise, a Saint Paul budget analyst at the time. And finally, my wife, Florence, who made the day possible through her guidance, leadership and patience throughout my City Hall career.

My only regrets were that my ma and pa weren't there. They lived on the street for 42 years.

CHAPTER 83

Now Comes the End

ONE JANUARY DAY IN 1987, I was at Mass at Saint Ambrose Church, my church for 65 years. John Ricci, my first City Hall deputy who was also a member, told me he was retiring June 30.

I was stunned. I was only 65, and John was even younger, 58.

It's a screwup in the pension plan, John said. The Professional Employees Retirement Association had made a mistake and overpaid into our retirement accounts. Rather than try to get members to repay the fund, the plan would not increase its contributions for the next two years.

So there I was—what do you do now, big boy? I had planned to run forever. You can get the feel when you're in trouble, like I was during my third election, but I didn't have that feeling yet. However, I was starting to be on the fence.

I had just been elected in 1986 to my 11th two-year term. I was going to be 65 in May. If I stayed on and retired in 1989, my pension would be no better than I would get if I retired right away.

After much deliberation and discussions with my wife and children, I decided to retire with many, many of my longtime City Hall friends.

One problem: finding a replacement for the last six months for my position. I talked to all of the council members, who had to approve my replacement. Who was more qualified and deserving than Eileen Wieda, the neighborhood activist who was well-liked and knew her way around City Hall. And it was well-known she was dying of cancer, so the appointment wouldn't encourage a person with long-term political ambitions.

The council appointed Eileen, who did a very credible job as my replacement. A feisty person, she once wore Army fatigues to a council meeting, stating she was "ready for battle."

She was an upbeat person to her dying day, which became a reality shortly after the end of her term.

Tom Diamond was elected to replace her by the voters of the Seventh Ward to represent them. Susie Vanelli remained as the aide.

CHAPTER 84

Checking the Record

IN MY POLITICAL CAREER I don't feel I set the world on fire, but I did work hard.

Probably the most important thing I did was help in that last push to save the old Federal Courts from demolition—and from that came the Landmark Center. I would like to think I was one of the best Parks and Rec commissioner in the city's history. Among other things, I welcomed the beginnings of the Minnesota Zoo instead of fighting its coming into being, as previous Parks commissioners had done. I helped institute bartender rights for women—after a first failure in January 1969 to give women the right to tend bar, they did eventually get that right in Saint Paul. Deputy Mike Sirian got compost locations established, and my office worked to establish new programs for entertainment at Como Park.

'He's Got a Point There, Vic. No Woman Bartender Could Do That.'

I also was involved in starting the Saint Patrick's Day parade and the

Taste of Minnesota at the State Capitol. But full credit for "Taste" goes to Ron Maddox, who ran with the idea for it.

One of my ideas that came to pass, at least in a small way, was to have a Minnesota Hall of Fame in the capital city of Saint Paul. An ideal location was the Union Depot. I wanted to go to International Falls and get a footprint of Bronko Nagurski, a fullback legend with the University of Minnesota Gophers and in the 1930s, with the Chicago Bears. Then we could add Vice President Hubert Humphrey, Vikings Coach Bud Grant, actress Judy Garland—the list would have been endless. But I couldn't get anyone interested. Finally, under Mayor George Latimer, we did put four footprints at the entrance of the Depot in May 1986. But neither George nor I remember who they were, and in 2005, they have already disappeared.

CHAPTER 85

Sending Out Thank-Yous

I'M GOING TO MAKE THE CARDINAL SIN of thanking some people while I know I'll be forgetting others. Bill Godwin, owner of a hardware store at Payne and Maryland—if there was something going on Payne Avenue or Arcade Street he was involved in it. And more often than not I was also—at his behest. Polly Hecht and Marlyn Trevino of the Eastsider newspaper—they were the newspaper. Don Boxmeyer, Karl Karlson, Don Del Fiacco of the *Saint Paul Pioneer Press Dispatch*—straightforward reporters and not of the "gotcha" mode. And I can't forget to mention Stan Turner of KSTP-TV.

And the musicians through the years who performed with me at senior high-rises, picnics, rec parties and always gratis. The appearances helped me and did nothing for them. I got the glory—perhaps they got satisfaction. First of all Dick Kadrie, he played so many. Clarence Sowers, Fred Kahle, Gerald Brockway, Gerry Sognesond, Andy Ciccarella, Nick Campobasso, Bill Durand, Russell Ek, Lenny Chickett and his wife, Marlys, and many others too numerous to mention.

CHAPTER 86

Waving Good-bye

THE FINAL STEP IN MY POLITICAL LIFE was my retirement party—and what a party it was. We had 893 people in attendance at $25 apiece, and had very little money left after expenses. What little there was went for a final party for my volunteer workers throughout the years.

Lt. Gov. Marlene Johnson was the principal speaker. My third mayor, Larry Cohen, was MC. Father Pingatore of my longtime church, Saint Ambrose, gave the opening blessing. Rabbi Zielengol of Adath Israel, an Orthodox synagogue, gave the benediction. We had become friends after I met the rabbi through my former business partner, Willie Olmer.

There were monkeys and snakes from the zoo. We had a 15-piece dance band, which played gratis for me. I got gifts, plaques, what have you. What a party, what a night—I couldn't believe it was all for me.

My wife, Florence, was in attendance, as were my children Patricia, Elizabeth and Tony, and Pat's husband, Bill Bloyer, and my grandchildren, Justin and Kirstin, who were devastated because I retired. My sister, Mary, and her husband, Alfred Gentile; my brother Nick and his wife, Helen; my brother Albert and his wife-to-be, Linda, were there. Phyllis and Tom Ethier—Phyllis had volunteered many hours of time, being the main organizer of the event. So many people, so many well-wishers.

The morning preceding the party at the Civic Center, we had food stands at Rice Park—opened at 7 in the morning. Hundreds of people throughout the day stopped by to have coffee and doughnuts. At City Hall were two big cakes in the foyer beneath the statue, "The God of Peace." Council members were cutting cake for the visitors. Upstairs in the Council Chambers, the last council meeting for Councilman Vic Tedesco started about 10:30 A.M. It was sad. Justin was in tears, Kirstin was in tears, I was in tears, others were in tears.

I think I was most touched by council member Kikki Sonnen when she said that day, "Vic Tedesco is a man of humor and a man of honor."

The biggest, happiest part of my life was behind me.

My grandchildren, Kirstin and Justin Bloyer, were very unhappy that I was leaving the City Council. Mayor George Latimer gave me a good send-off.
Star Tribune/Minneapolis-St. Paul 2005

PART FIVE

Retiring to Music

CHAPTER 87

From Politician to Lobbyist

I MAY HAVE BEEN RETIRED, but I didn't stop working. I became a lobbyist.

My office was on the first floor of a building I bought at 750 E. Seventh St. on Saint Paul's East Side. It was a fourplex with two commercial units downstairs and two living units upstairs. I called it the Florence Building, of course after my wife, Florence. I tried to buy the small apartment building next door and call it the Florence Apartments, but the deal didn't work out.

The District 4 Community Council was being evicted from their location, so they moved into the office across from mine on the first floor. The two residents on the second floor were nice, but one had a big, big dog. The neighbors in the apartment building next door were complaining about the barking, so I had to tell the young lady she'd have to move. I told her she could have a couple months to relocate. She left and we parted friends. In fact, we exchanged Christmas cards for the next 15 years.

I moved upstairs into her vacant unit. It was so much nicer. I had a big bay window with a nice view of the open space at the Wilder senior citizens' campus across the street.

One day my dear friend Carmen Tuminelly came to visit me. He and I go back to the days before World War II, and Florence and I and he and his wife, Dar, socialized through the years. One of the best home and office builders, he had retired. He built the golf clubhouse for Hillcrest Country Club on Larpenteur Avenue, a beautiful structure. He also built our first home at 2160 Larry Ho Drive, which was and is the nicest home in the neighborhood. With regrets, we had sold it—it became too big for just two people.

Carmen and I sat chatting and he started assessing the office, saying, we can build a bookcase here and an Italian door here. I told him I didn't want to spend that kind of money. He said, won't cost you much, and he was right. He didn't want any money—I paid him a token payment, and I mean token. By the time Carmen got done, the place was a palace—it was a pleasure to come to work there.

My first client was Liberty Bank. They wanted someone to watch over their rezoning for a parking lot next door. I got $500, plus they gave me the fence around the empty lot they were rezoning. I used the fencing around my property at 750—it worked out perfectly for me and I felt I did a good job for the bank.

Pier 1 was another account I had—their situation was much more difficult, having to do with a rezoning to expand their building on Grand Avenue. The neighbors were adamant against the rezoning—they didn't want more commercialization on their street, and they fought every inch of the way. After two months I knew I couldn't help them, so rather than stringing them along, I told them that and dropped the account.

My third account was Angelo Vitali. He wanted a bar transfer. I had known Angelo all my life; he used to run with my older brother Nick, and I worked for him a short time after the war. He got the bar transfer, but I'm sure he could have gotten it without my help.

I quit lobbying after six months. I didn't like the constant ass-kissing to keep the client happy.

CHAPTER 88

From Bleach to Vinyl

It wasn't the first time I'd had to give up on a business, but at least this time it was my choice. Both *Touchdown USA,* the football newspaper I started just after Nick and I sold WISK radio, and Donna Jayne's wig shop just plain went under.

In the mid-1960s, I tried selling bleach. Dream-X was a home bleach product similar to Clorox. I was in business with my boyhood pals Dan Pilla and Matt Morelli—Matt would say, "Not of the grocery family—I'm the poor one."

There were three Morelli families in Little Italy—and not related. They weren't even distant cousins. When Matt spoke of the rich Morelli, he meant Matt Morelli, owner of Morelli's Grocery and Liquors, one of the largest and busiest liquor stores. That Matt also owned a bar and a pizza restaurant. He was very successful, but he worked hard night and day.

The third Morelli family lived on East Minnehaha Avenue, just on the western edge of Little Italy. I knew two brothers in the family, George and Mike. George died many years ago, but Mike is a dear friend who, with my brother-in-law, Al Gentile, put up most of my political lawn signs over the years.

The Matt I was in the bleach business with was a city employee with the water department. He, Dan and I were selling bleach out of a storefront on East Seventh Street for 25 cents a gallon, in your own jug. The cost of the bleach was nominal and rent was cheap; it was the plastic jugs that killed you. They cost 22.5 cents each, a big chunk of expense that hurt profits.

We were doing quite well on a minimal investment when

along came a manufacturer's representative who talked us into going "big time." We bought a used semi and rented a lot of space a block away from Hi-Lex on the West Side. All this because we got a big contract to furnish Super-Valu stores with bleach. And that we did. Truckload after truckload. Before we knew it, we were in deep trouble financially. I sold out to Dan Pilla for one dollar. He did me a big favor. The company eventually went out of business.

My nephew, Bobby Hegner, was a real talent and it's a shame he didn't get anywhere in the entertainment business. But I knew many talented people in the music business who never got that one break.

One of the songs Bobby wrote was "18 Wheels of Hell," a country-Western song about loving the open road. I thought it was good, to the point that I sponsored the making of a record of it in 1978. Bobby and his wife, Laurie, and me and my son, Tony, went to Nashville to cut the record.

CHAPTER 89

"18 Wheels of Hell"

CHARTWHEEL WAS THE LABEL. I had enough of a musical background to know that it was a professional, well-done recording. We had two good female background singers and five musicians. One of the guys was named Leroy and was the lead guitarist for Ernie Tubb, who always said on his records, "Take 'er away, Leroy." By the time they redubbed the vocalists and musicians, it sounded like a choir group and a 15-piece country band.

I thought it was a great record—"18 Wheels" on one side and on the flip side, Bobby sang two Jerry Lee Lewis classics, "Whole Lot of Shakin' Goin' On" and "Great Balls of Fire." Cost me $3,000 and I felt it was worth it.

The record got plenty of exposure—Mel Jass and Nancy Nelson of Channel 11, WTCN-TV, gave us a good shot. KTCR-FM, the country-Western station, gave us much, much playtime—thanks to my brother Albert, who owned the station.

Heilicher Bros., a powerful record distributor, wanted 500 copies, so we ordered them. Two days later Heilicher's called back and said they had changed their mind. For some time, I had 500 copies of "18 Wheels of Hell" sitting next to thousands of copies of *Touchdown USA* in my garage. And one bottle of Dream-X bleach.

CHAPTER 90

"Vic's Vintage Videos"

I AM A DREAMER. I like to dwell in the past. My office was a place to display my collection of 21 scrapbooks from my City Council days, my photos, memorabilia, LP record collection and videotape collection.

I had loved movies since I was a kid. One of my prize possessions is a VHS copy of the 12 chapters of "Hurricane Express," the John Wayne serial I watched week after week at the State Theater. Eventually I found it on DVD, too.

My office was also the base for the Aïda Film Co., named after my mama.

It was part of "Vic's Vintage Videos," my cable TV show that started just before I left the City Council. It seems I always found a second use for something I was involved in. All that research in the early 1980s when I was on the City Council had gotten me interested in cable TV, and now I was producing my own public-access show at Suburban Community cable TV in White Bear Lake.

I was still on the city council, but almost retired. The young lady in charge of the program, a Ms. Jackson, was excellent—knew the rudiments of putting a TV show on the air. We taped a new introduction for each show, usually three or four at a time. I would bring several sport coats and change between tapings so the viewers didn't think I had only one coat.

I was renting films from a company in Kansas City for $60 a show. I found out the films were in the public domain, that is, the copyright had run out, and the movies belonged to the public. They could be run free of charge; therefore, I had no film charges for my show. I built up quite a library of old movies on VHS tape; now I find them for sale on DVDs at bargain stores. The distributors for these DVDs clearly note that package design is under copyright, letting you think the movie is copyrighted. But it isn't—and they must be making a fortune.

CHAPTER 91

Down to the Basement

A<small>T FIRST I WAS VERY HAPPY</small> with the Florence Building. From my picture window I could see Swede Hollow, where I was born. We left there when I was only two years old, but when I was a boy on Collins Street, I visited the Hollow quite often to see friends, even through high school days.

But soon I became disillusioned with my little building as the neighborhood began to deteriorate.

I spent $700 for a canvas canopy to dress up the front of the building. Someone ripped it up, and the fence was wrecked, too. Each morning I had to clean up the trash in my yard and in the alley behind my yard. Many teenage parties took place there during the wee hours. I decided to sell the building and move on.

I transferred the offices of Vic's Vintage Videos and Aïda Films to the basement of my home. In 1988, I added to the mix a cable TV talk show.

I had been racking my brain trying to come up with a name for it. One day Florence and I were with our friend Joann Spindler, visiting her mother, Ellen, up at Garrison, Minn., when I talked about not being able to find a name for the show. Joann suggested, why not call it "TNT—Tedesco in Touch," and we did.

"Vic's Vintage Videos" soon bit the dust, but I continue to tape "Tedesco 'n Touch." For the unscripted shows, I interviewed Bill Veeck, owner of the minor-league Saint Paul Saints; boxer Scott LeDoux; Al Baisi, a Chicago Bears guard in the 1940s; famous Twin Cities Italian cook Mama D; Medusa, a beautiful lady wrestler; former Mayor Larry Cohen when he had just been appointed a Ramsey County district judge; and many others.

Medusa, who used only a first name professionally, gave me a large poster of herself in her wrestling shorts and top. I displayed it on the wall of my office library until the day I moved. Sorry, no room at home for Medusa.

I also interviewed Kay McDaniel and Jean Havlish, who were members of the All-American Girls Professional Baseball League during World War II. The league got a boost of fame in 1992 with the movie, "A League of Their Own." Kay lived in Rosemount at the time of the interview, and Jean was a housekeeper for a priest in the Saint Cloud area. After baseball, Jean became a professional bowler and has a 300 game to her credit. They were both great athletes, but more important, they were both great ladies. I was really impressed with both of them.

I continue to do the show as of this writing.

CHAPTER 92

The Big Band Swings Again

I ALSO GOT BACK INTO THE BAND BUSINESS and started booking my small and big band. After Randy Kelly was elected mayor of Saint Paul in 2001, we started performing together at senior citizens' homes. I would play my sax and he would play guitar and sing. He does both quite well.

Before his election, Randy told senior citizens that he would be there to entertain them. Yes, we have been back to every senior citizen center where he said he would play. He is one genuine guy—a man of his word. I've only met two, Randy and Gov. Rudy Perpich.

After quitting lobbying, I did some work for Perpich as a senior ombudsman. I was a goodwill ambassador, going before seniors throughout the state promoting Minnesota 1990, a program saluting cities throughout the state. I visited Sleepy Eye, Darwin, Mora and many other towns. I was good for the promotion with my backgrounds in broadcasting and politics, and most of all, my rapport with seniors.

I continue to entertain at senior events. Every time I play "Let the Rest of the World Go By," I remember Florence Hargins at the USO in Frankfort, Ky., and I give her special recognition.

I play some events gratis, some not. I will not entertain gratis at a nursing home where the residents pay $5,000 to $6,000 a month to stay. I've done at least 1,000 free gigs for worthy causes. Sometimes if I'm lucky I get $85, of which $60 goes to my accordian player, Nancy Lovegren, and the rest goes to gasoline and the upkeep of my instruments.

And I really got back into the big-band business. At first we were playing 50 to 60 shows a year, but more recently I've settled on about 30 shows in 10 months.

Each August I have a big band concert at the Phipps Theater in Hudson, Wis. This event is the entertainment highlight of the year for me.

I lead a 17-piece dance band with musicians I never dreamt in my life I would be on the same stage with. The vocalist, Debbie Bigelow, is a delight—great vocalist, great entertainer, great person. In addition to Debbie, we have a vocal quartet in the manner of the Pied Pipers with the Tommy Dorsey Orchestra or the Modernaires with the Glenn Miller Orchestra. And to top it off, I get Stan Turner, former longtime anchorman at KSTP-TV, to introduce us.

I enjoy bringing music to people. Star Tribune/ Minneapolis-St. Paul 2005

The big band has also played at the Minnesota State Fair, Ramsey County Fair, outdoor concerts at Lindstrom, Chisago City, Chaska, Crystal, Hastings, Hudson and Saint Paul. One of our select engagements is the Taste of Minnesota on the Fourth of July each year.

At the Taste, I have had the pleasure of appearing with Patti Page, Pat Boone, Myron Floren and the Count Basie Band. At a senior citizens' event on Harriet Island, I was the "straight man"

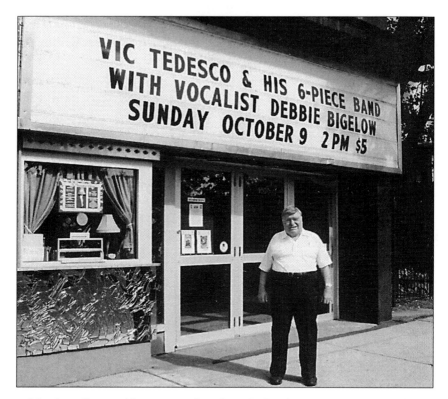

I lead small ensembles at many locations. In October 2005, vocalist Debbie Bigelow was along as we played the Mounds Theater on Saint Paul's East Side.

for Henny Youngman, famous comedian. He's really caustic. I didn't care for him on or off stage.

In the summer of 1997, I led a smaller ensemble, only seven pieces, for background music on QVC, one of the cable-television shopping networks. To avoid having to play royalties, we played all music that wasn't copyrighted, old favorites such as "My Old Kentucky Home."

I even directed the Lawrence Welk band once. It was in October 2003, when I traveled to Branson, Mo., with my friend Daniel Szlapski, a delight to be with. I first met Welk, who died in 1992, back in the 1930s when I was selling newspapers outside the Saint Paul Hotel. Then his band was called the Hotsie-Totsies; the band in Branson is modeled after the Champagne

Music Makers on his popular TV show in the 1950s and 1960s, "The Lawrence Welk Show."

Dan and I were enjoying a performance of the Lawrence Welk band at the Lawrence Welk Champagne Theatre in Branson, Mo., when the bandleader, James Hobson, called for volunteers from the audience to direct the musicians, and I volunteered. It was a fun experience, and the bandleader told me I did a good job directing. I wanted to tell him I had done it many times before, but I didn't want to sound flippant.

I was so fortunate to play with some great local musicians— too many to mention them all. One of my favorites was Fred Kahle, who was band director at South Saint Paul High School. He played trombone and violin, excelled in both, but most important, he was a fine, decent man. He died in February 2001. Joe de Marco was a fine tenor sax man, and Joe Fercello on alto sax. Both of them played with me in my earlier days. Bob Gruenfelder was great on trumpet. I played with him several times but had to quit. He was a chain-smoker and I'd get sick. It just wasn't worth it.

Roger (Buzz) Peterson, who joined my band about 1995, made a lasting impression as an excellent trumpet player. He had worked with Gene Autry on his radio show in 1954 and played in many fine bands in the Twin Cities area. He played his last date on Jan. 13, 2005, adding his horn to a four-piece band led by me at a dance for senior citizens at the Gladstone Community Center in Maplewood. Less than six months later, Buzz was buried.

Marvin Rechtzigel was really special. He and I played together for 40 years. We played so many bookings together that on one occasion when he was very unhappy with a guitarist I had hired, he told me if I ever hired that guy again, he didn't want to play with us. Marv was kind of grumpy, but he was so genuine and really a lovable guy.

He started playing the accordian when he was four years old. He was the son of a farmer; did his chores, went to school and at the end of a busy day practiced his accordian for three to four hours each night. Marv's last engagement was a house party in Woodbury in May 2004. It was just the two of us, me on saxophone and him on accordian. He died on my birthday, May 22, 2005.

Bob Stacke, then band director at Armstrong High School in Bloomington, played drums. In 1985, Bob got a position with a symphony orchestra in Caracas, Venezuela. He was gung ho to move, was going to sell his house in Minneapolis. I told him, don't do it. Go down there and get the feel of the situation.

At the end of the year he was back. The money was good, but it made him nervous to see soldiers stationed throughout the theater with machine guns. He was glad he didn't sell his house. He went back to Armstrong, and played drums at Chanhassen Dinner Theatre for years.

CHAPTER 93

Faith and Saint Ambrose

ALL THE BUSINESSES THAT FLOURISHED in Little Italy when I was young are gone, except for Morelli's, now a large supermarket run by the third generation, Jimmy and Louie Morelli. The triangle of land where Machovec's grocery and Leonard's Bar stood is now a vacant lot with flowers and a sign welcoming people to Railroad Island. That's the name today for Little Italy.

Until 1998, Saint Ambrose Catholic Church, where I had belonged all my life, was there in Little Italy.

My faith in God is important to me. Each night my prayer list contains 258 names. It's like a roll call in an Army camp or a school. I remember little Serafina, my sister who died in Italy before my mother immigrated. I pray for both sets of grandparents, none of whom I got to meet. And I pray for my living family members and so many of my friends.

For many years, Florence and I would visit seven churches on Holy Thursday during Lent, riding on a tour bus arranged by Nick Cucchiarella, the one we called "Bishop" when we were kids. The destinations changed each year, and ranged from the cathedral in Saint Cloud to a little country church at the crossroads of two county roads. I don't think it could seat even 100 people.

I have also tried to live my faith by serving my church. I was a reader, or lector, for 21 years at Saint Ambrose and an usher for as long as I can remember. I was a trustee for 17 years, with Matt Morelli of the grocery store being the other trustee.

Saint Ambrose started as a missionary church, a branch of Holy Redeemer Catholic Church in downtown Saint Paul (Florence's parish). Father Louis Pioletti, the one who used to pull my ears when I was young, was the priest and Father Thomas Pingatore was his assistant. In 1956, Saint Ambrose was named a national parish, or ethnic parish, for Italians, and Father Pingatore its priest.

Churches aren't usually designated for ethnic groups now, but at the time, other national churches included Holy Cross, a Polish church in Minneapolis, Assumption in Saint Paul for Germans and Saint Casimir in Saint Paul for Poles. Priests usually stay at a national parish for a lifetime, and Father Pingatore did just that for the Italian Saint Ambrose.

As a trustee of Saint Ambrose, I was considered just a "yes man" to Father Pingatore by some Saint Ambrose parishioners. If being a "yes man" meant reviewing maintenance contracts for repairs, approving a new roof, snowplowing, etc., then I guess I was a "yes man."

Father Thomas Pingatore, who died in 2005, was my dear friend and spiritual advisor for more than 50 years.

The parish ran into difficulties as the demographics of the neighborhood changed. One morning about 1997 we came out after Mass and saw five police cars at Burr Street and Minnehaha Avenue, their lights flashing as the officers investigated some disturbance. Occasionally when the church windows and doors were open you could hear the neighbors swearing and yelling out cuss words.

Attendance started to drop dramatically. Some parishioners wanted to close the church. Some wanted to start a new parish. Poor Father Pingatore, the only priest the people of Saint Ambrose had ever had—he was caught in the middle.

He suggested moving Saint Ambrose to the fast-growing Saint Paul suburb of Woodbury. The new congregation was established in April 1998, and the doors to the old Saint Ambrose closed on May 31, 1998.

The move was disastrous. Some parishioners accused him of "selling out" and to this day many of the worshipers from the city parish felt they were not accepted by the parishoners of the relocated church in Woodbury. At the old Saint Ambrose, the average age of the congregants was about 70, I'd say. At the new Saint Ambrose, it's 4, yes, 4. I guess young families and old-timers don't mix, at least not in this case.

Many Saint Ambrose parishioners transferred to Saint John's at 977 E. Fifth St., Saint Paul, to follow Father Pingatore. Although my membership stayed with Saint Ambrose, I started attending Saint John's also and became a reader.

Some people felt Father Pingatore betrayed them with the move, but in my opinion, he had no choice.

I visited him in June 2005 in Saint Joseph's Hospital in Saint Paul after he had had a stroke. It was sad to see my longtime friend so helpless. He died just five days later.

I hate hospital visits—but they've got to be done!!!

CHAPTER 94

Walking Around

THE LORD HAS BEEN SO GOOD TO ME. He gave me fairly good health in my retirement years. Fortunately, I love to walk.

While in City Hall, many mornings I would walk to work from Third and White Bear Avenue to downtown Saint Paul, 4.5 miles, to be exact. People would stop and offer me a ride. I'd say, no, thank you—I need the exercise. After retirement, I would walk in Battle Creek Park at McKnight Road North and Upper Afton Road. Once around the three little ponds was 1.3 miles. Some days I would walk around them three times.

I got to meet so many nice people there. On several occasions we had a breakfast party at Keys, a local cafe, with 12 to 15 people. So many nice people—though I can hardly remember their names. One nice lady was a volunteer at the Minnesota Zoo. Jim King, about 6 feet, and his wife, Helen, no taller than 5 feet, were a delightful couple, as were Archie and Ginny Raines. Germaine Schaeffer and Sue Dean were regulars, as was Jerry D'Aloia. Germaine had her dog Mort along, and Jerry his dog, but I forgot his name. Linda Schulte and I talked about our lives during our walks—I don't know what became of her.

CHAPTER 95

The Health-Club Scene

W ILLIE OLMER, MY FORMER REAL ESTATE business partner, kept nagging me about joining a health club. Willie said he was a survivor of the Holocaust, that he spent time in Buchenwald. He couldn't read or write—but he became a millionaire six times over.

"Victa,"—he had a very heavy Jewish accent—"you join the club, you meet lotsa pretty ladies." At his insistence I joined the Carlton Health Club, but I didn't meet many ladies, pretty or not.

I couldn't believe how inexpensive it was: $87 for the year. But I did not socialize at the Carlton, which was out of character for me. Usually I went there with Willie. Not too many people took a liking to him—he had a strong personality. Sometimes he drove me nuts with his antics. He would brag to a waitress about how successful he was and how much money he had, and then leave her a little dollar tip.

When the Carlton was sold to the Minnesota Mining Co. for an exclusive 3M fitness club, the remainder of the contract was honored at the Woodbury Golf and Fitness Club, but Willie didn't join there. Eventually, he developed Alzheimer's disease. I really felt sorry for him. He died in 2003. I never thought I'd see the day I would miss him, but I do. He was unique.

It's funny in life, just when you think something has gone bad the next step makes you glad. When I left the broadcasting business I thought it was the end of the world and yet the political life was more enjoyable, more satisfying. Now I had lost a health club, but Woodbury Fitness was an improvement for me. It introduced me to the happiest period of my retirement life.

Immediately I began to meet nice people. The very first day I met Judy Cohoon and Andrea Davis, both attractive blondes. At first I couldn't distinguish between the two of them. I'd say, "Good morning, Judy," and she'd say, "I'm Andrea," and with Andrea the same thing. Michele Dahlberg, assistant manager when I joined, was always upbeat, with a smile at all times. I met a lot of nice guys, too, like Dan Patrick, a "class guy" who's a retired schoolteacher and a dear friend, Rick Davis, Rev. Ralph Olsen of King of Kings Lutheran Church, and Chris Scullen.

But Woodbury Golf and Fitness got into financial trouble when Lifetime Fitness moved into the area. Woodbury was a delight—small, and like the saying on the "Cheers" TV show, it was a place "where everybody knows your name." When you don't own the business it's easy to second-guess its future—I

In 1991, my friends at Woodbury Golf and Fitness Club threw me a birthday party.

Another birthday party, this one with friends from
Lifetime Fitness and elsewhere.

thought Woodbury could weather the competitive storm, but it
didn't. It closed and we all ended up at Lifetime, which cost twice
as much as Woodbury. Now it's $50 a month, almost three times
as much as the small Woodbury club.

Just as several times before in my lifetime, something I thought
was going to be a bad deal for me turned out just the opposite.
Lifetime was just great. Many of the friends I made at Woodbury
transferred to Lifetime, including Jodi Sward, Laura Moore, Barb
Navarro, Rick Davis, Henri and Mary Jo Buffalo, the Rev. Ralph
Olsen of King of Kings Lutheran Church. Others included Sheri
Singer, who's my swimming instructor, Susan Dickhudt, Karen
Peterson, Barb Bryant, Donna Lande and Sigred Meyers.

I made so many new friendships at Lifetime also—the new
friends include Lyn Olson, Jan Ekmark, Nancy Annette, Jim Con-
roy, Doug Scheerer, Milt Klohn, Jerry Ethier. Debbie Long became

a close friend who organized my 80th birthday party. Dan Szlapski and I have taken trips together. Another dear friend, Pat Richmond, left Lifetime to go to the YMCA in Hudson.

All the friends I met at my health clubs were friendly, compatible people with whom it was a pleasure to talk for an hour or two several days a week. Many have also become social friends of Florence and mine, going out for lunch or dinner.

I could go on and on with lists of friends. I'll bet I know 300 people, maybe more, on a first-name basis—and that I consider to be so fortunate for me.

—— CHAPTER 96 ——

Retired, but Hardly Retiring

I JUST LOVED PEOPLE. I would go to jazz and big-band concerts with my dear friend Mike Sirian, who served as my assistant at City Hall.

In the early 1980s, Mayor Latimer asked me to sub for him at Saint Paul Night sponsored by the Minnesota Twins in the Metrodome. I had the duty of throwing out the first pitch. I was awful. The ball hit home plate instead of the catcher's glove.

Tony Oliva, the Twins' former star outfielder who was acting as Twins commentator that night for the broadcast on WCCO-TV, said it was the worst first pitch he'd ever seen thrown out in his lifetime. I got a lot of heat about my pitching prowess, but I had fun and got a lot of compliments from the fans. Willie Olmer, who was with me, got a lot of paraphernalia, hats and glove, etc.

In 2002 I was going to have my 80th birthday party with about 20 people attending. I made the mistake of inviting Debbie Long, a friend from Lifetime Fitness. She thought reaching the age of 80 was quite an achievement and we should have a bigger party. I wish I had known her when I was in politics—what an organizer.

With Debbie in charge, and with the help of Ruth Krieger, Cici Szcech, Linda Napton and others, the party grew to 144 people at Clyde's on the River in Bayport. Stan Turner, who became the news director of Minnesota News Network (64 stations) after his long stint as anchorman at KSTP-TV, was the MC. Debbie Bigelow, from my big band, was the vocalist, with

Dean Kleven, pianist. My guests gave me a beautiful engraved gold watch and many nice gifts.

I found out later that Debbie Long does a lot of charity work, especially for animal rights. Maybe she's influenced by her three cats, Sailor, Missy and Rascal.

CHAPTER 97

On the Road with Ed

WHAT A DEAR FRIEND I HAVE HAD in Ed Eberhardt, who was director of the Health Department for the city of Saint Paul. We have gone on about two short trips a year for many years. Destinations have included Huntsville, Ala., and to Houston to see the space centers there, and Chicago, to visit my wartime friend Mary Haney Freundt.

About 2002, we decided to make our visit to Mary the start of a trip to visit the graves of some of my wartime buddies. Though we had visited her often after Herb died in the mid 1990s, I had never been to see his grave. She took us to a cemetery about five miles from her home. It was so huge we had trouble finding the grave. It had just a small headstone with his name.

Next we headed for Yonkers, N.Y., where my friend Tony Polidore is buried. What a crappy town—cars parked in the middle of the street, crowds milling everywhere, looking as if they were looking for trouble. It wasn't like peaceful, clean Saint Paul.

Tony never served on the same base with me; we met at the USO in Frankfort. He was probably the only soldier I knew who was shorter than me. He was also of Italian descent and aways had a smile on his chubby face.

We went to a fire station to get directions to St. Genevieve Cemetery, but they couldn't help. Said there was no cemetery by that name in Yonkers. We spent about two hours trying to reach Tony's nephew and niece by phone before we gave up and headed for our next stop, Rochester, N.H., where Carl Sprich was buried.

Carl was a buddy at Fort Knox. He slept in the next bunk over from me. I took him up to the USO in Frankfort, but he didn't hit it off with any of the women—his girl, Betty, was waiting at home for him. We went to a funeral home for directions to the gravesite. No luck. Finally I called his daughter in Virginia and she set us straight.

I called Carl's widow, Betty, whom I had never met. Ed and I took her to lunch and then headed for Carl's grave. They say opposites attract, and this must have been the case with Carl and Betty. He was a very quiet guy; if you were going to have a conversation with him, you had to start it yourself. Betty was just the opposite—talkative as the day is long. I wonder if Carl ever got a word in.

Ed often went with me to Frankfort, Ky., where I had so many fun times in the Army 60-plus years ago. I still have a photograph in my office at home of the 19 young ladies who were volunteers who started the USO club.

I have visited my friends in Frankfort about every five years—though the number had shrunk from 19 to 6 at the time of my last visit in August 2003. One of my favorites, Alma La Fontaine, lives in Daytona Beach, Fla., with her husband, Maurice, and her grandson, Justin Boughton. My brother Nick lived in Daytona Beach so over the years I got to see Alma and her family several times.

Only a few USO girls from World War II remain in Frankfort, Ky. About 2002, they and some of their friends gathered with me for a reunion.

Ed and I went to a reunion of the 10th Armored Division Association—I'm a member—about 1998 in Birmingham, Ala. Our unit revisited Fort Benning, Ga., on a guided tour; we visited "Sand Hill" where I was stationed in 1943. Don't remember the exact building I was in, but I saw similar buildings. We had lunch in an ultra-modern building—not an Army barracks like we had.

Ed and I visited Tuxedo Junction in Birmingham, Ala. Being a musician, I was familiar with the lyrics about dancing the night away Southern style, in the song that was recorded by Glenn Miller in 1940. I was so disappointed. The junction was a street corner with a big rock with a plaque on it. To me it was a "nothing" scene, about as exciting as Sixth and Jackson in downtown Saint Paul.

I'm also a member of the 69th Infantry Division Association. When it scheduled its 60th reunion in Louisville for September 2005, Ed knew he wouldn't go along. July 2005 would see his 88th birthday, and he was staying pretty close to home. My only surviving buddy in the 69th, Alex Lassiegne, has Alzheimer's disease and wouldn't be attending. Eventually, I too decided to stay home.

It turned out to be a good decision as Hurricane Katrina, which decimated much of Louisiana, Mississippi and Alabama at the end of August 2005, caused flooding in Louisville as it tracked north.

CHAPTER 98

Cotronei Revisited

In 1989, my brother Nick, my sister Mary and I went to Italy to spend time in Cotronei, Italy, the hometown of our mother and father. Florence and I had stopped there on our 1971 trip to Italy, but this visit was to be devoted to our Italian relatives.

The village had grown from the 1,400 people of our parents' time to about 6,000 in 1989, but it still didn't have a train station. We were met at a village about 20 miles away by a cousin, who drove us to the village. We kept going up and up, higher and higher, into the mountains.

In the town, we were met by several cousins. One of them, an attractive widow, wanted the three of us to stay with her. Her home was beautiful and more than adequate for all of us. But another cousin wanted us to stay with him and his wife—and said that if we didn't, we would shame him as he had told everyone we were his guests.

So we stayed there, but it wasn't a successful arrangement. Nick and I shared a guest bed. Mary slept in our hosts' bed while they slept on couches. Also in the household were two young teenagers, their grandchildren who were living with them. They were very nice, well-behaved kids, but the house was barely big enough for our hosts and the two grandkids, and it was sure was full with seven of us for five nights.

Cotronei reminded me of American small towns of the 1930s. They had small grocery stores on almost every block, one bank and one church—Catholic, and the center of the town. The water was shut off from noon until 6 P.M. every day. People would fill their bathtubs with water in case they needed some during that time.

I had so many relatives there, it got to be overwhelming. They smothered us with kindness. We couldn't spend a nickel. To show our appreciation, we threw a going away party at a local restaurant. We told our host to invite our relatives. We thought there would be 20 to 25 people—there were 80, and that was with only a day's notice.

CHAPTER 99

A Lifetime of Friends

I HAVE NO SURVIVING BUDDIES in the 10th Armored, and only Alex Lasseigne in the 69th Infantry. But I have a lifetime of memories from so many years and so many places and so many friends.

In addition to Lasseigne I have one other buddy, Charlie Simone, in Philadelphia. I wanted to meet him half way, in Cleveland, two years ago. But he said, "Vic I have arthritis so bad I can't go around the block."

Many years after I "danced with Dolly with a hole in her stocking," back when I was in Louisville, Ky., for my stateside war service, her husband, Al Colyard, and I became good friends back in Saint Paul, where we had grown up together in Little Italy. Dolly had died quite young. Al, who had been in the Merchant Marines, in recent years has been president of the Columbus Memorial Association, an Italian-American group to which I also belong.

Jimmy Atria, another wartime buddy, became a successful apartment-building owner in Florida, corresponded with me for years. I got together with him on one of my trips to Daytona Beach, Fla. I used to drive to Daytona with my brother Albert, who had a winter residence there, a condo on the Atlantic Ocean. Stuart, Fla., where Jimmy lived, was only 60 miles or so from there.

I would spend two weeks in early December with Albert and Nick, who was a Florida resident. Many a night we would spend at Nick and Helen's talking the evening away, reminiscing about the good old days, even though some of them weren't.

I enjoyed being with my brothers, sightseeing, a little night-clubbing and certainly enjoying the usually good weather. Then I would fly home to spend Christmas with my family.

CHAPTER 100

Finding a Fond Memory

I LOST TRACK OF TRUDI ROBERSON, the high school girl I dated while I was stationed at Fort Knox, when I was shipped to California. About 40 years later I wanted to see her one last time. I wrote to 18 Roberson families in the New Albany-Louisville area looking for her. I knew she had married and moved to Portland, Maine.

Several weeks later I got a letter from a young lady who was her third cousin and worked at the public library. She gave me Trudi's married name, address and phone number. Trudi's husband had died, and she had returned to New Albany, Ind.

I called her, and she was delighted to hear from me. I learned it would soon be her birthday so I sent her—guess what—an orchid corsage, without signing the card. She knew it was from me. It was only the second orchid corsage she had ever received, and both had come from me. We became good telephone pals until she remarried. I continued to send her cards and little mementos, but I never heard from her again.

I assume her new husband was quite protective, maybe even jealous—rather foolish in a man of 80-plus years. He had nothing to worry about. I went with four young ladies in my lifetime, all very nice girls, but I married the nicest one of the whole bunch.

— CHAPTER 101 —

Vic the Matchmaker

In my lifetime I brought together six couples.

Herb and Mary Freundt were the first couple I got to marry, back in Frankfort, Ky., during the war. After I came home to Saint Paul I started running with a lot of young people who would visit me while I was playing in a nightclub. Sometimes a couple of young ladies would ask me if I knew any nice guys. The light bulb would go on and I'd start matching people up.

About 1953, I was at Mounds Park Hospital after having my appendix removed. I was sharing a room with Thomas Schroepfer. Our nurse was a young lady named Jan from a small town in central Minnesota. He liked the nurse; she liked him. He was bashful; I was not. I went to work on them both. Florence and I were attendants at their wedding in 1954, and recently attended their 50th wedding anniversary party.

Next was Joe and Marion. Joe Fercello was a musician, a dear buddy of mine. We fixed him on a double date with Marion Leach about the same time as I was working on Tom and Jan. Marion was a supervisor at Northwestern Bell Telephone Co., a very nice-looking lady, very intelligent. They hit it off, married and had several children. Unfortunately Joe died rather young, in November 1983.

I continued my matchmaking streak with Emil Gatto and Rose Fischer. Emil worked at the railroad, and Rose at the telephone company with Marion. They were young—he handsome, she pretty, and both strong-willed. They shouldn't have hit it off, but they did, for more than 50 years. Emil died in February 2005.

The fifth couple was Lincoln Corbo and Stella Lanek. Stella was a lifelong friend of my wife's and Lincoln was a friend going back to our toddler days. They were attracted to each other, and, you guessed it, got married.

The sixth couple was Victor and Florence Tedesco.

All of us except Joe Fercello, who died so young, got to be married more than 50 years. I guess I can say I was a good matchmaker.

CHAPTER 102

Politics in the 21st Century

I TRY NOT TO GET POLITICALLY INVOLVED nowadays. Most of my friends are not only senior citizens, but in their 70s and 80s. And in most cases, my friends have become conservative, and some of them are staunch Democrats.

One said, "I'm a Democrat, not a DFLer," that hybrid party peculiar to Minnesota called the Democrat-Farmer-Labor Party.

I ran for office because I wanted to "be there" for people who needed help. But I've seen many liberal programs go to waste—individuals getting positions of importance at a nice salary while the program remains ineffective; individual clients milking the system; some programs worthy, others not.

As I got older and moved along in my political career, I changed from a liberal to a centrist Democrat. Many of my friends are Democrats who were loyal to me, and now I remain loyal to them.

I remain a Democrat although I find it difficult: I'm pro-life and I'm against same-sex marriage. But I have come to accept equal rights for homosexuals, and I'm against job discrimination of all kinds.

I'm not exactly enamoured with the Republicans, either. I feel I have nowhere to go for a political home.

I did help Randy Kelly get elected mayor of Saint Paul in 2001 and I supported him again in 2005. He and Gov. Rudy Perpich are two of the few politicians whose word was their bond.

In 2003 I attended Mayor Randy Kelly's state of the city talk at the beautiful Minnesota History Center in Saint Paul. He did an excellent job and was well-received.

I got a strange feeling sitting, looking at the crowd. It was packed with politicians and public figures, many of them friends of Kelly's. I knew only a handful. The stage was the same, the players, oh, so different.

So many of those who were active in the city have gone on, like Bill Godwin, who did so much for the Payne Avenue neighborhood. He died Sept. 1, 2005, and I went to his wake. Hardly anyone besides his family was there. Perhaps more folks showed up later.

It reminded me of another wake I attended and that was for Milton Rosen, who was the longest-serving City Council member in terms of number of years—32. His service was spread over about 50 years because he kept interrupting his council career to run for mayor, and always lost. Then he would run again for council and win, until Rosalie Butler defeated him for council in 1970.

I was the longest-serving council member who went undefeated, and late in 2005, I was the only living member from my first council of 1966.

At Rosen's wake, no one but me was there when I paid my respects, and it shocked me that people would forget him. But again, maybe more folks showed up later.

I left the funeral chapel, got into my car, turned the radio on, and there was Peggy Lee singing, "Is that all there is?"

Back in my City Hall days, any political gathering would have been very important to me. But those mostly empty wakes for once-popular politicians told an important story: The political game is nothing compared to what's the most important, and that's family.

CHAPTER 103

The Important Stuff in Life

I'VE BEEN TALKING ABOUT SO MANY PEOPLE in my life, but not much about the most important one, my dear wife, Florence.

Florence and I have been married for more than 58 years. What a blessing—the Lord sure was good to me when he gave me Florence.

She had just turned 18 when I married her. She was poor and I was poor, so she didn't marry me for wealth. She was and is a great mother—stay-at-home mom during our children's formative years. She brought up three, of whom we are extremely proud.

After the kids were grown she became a good business-woman, too, managing our rental property. She excelled in gardening, cooking and baking, and is much better at home repair than I am.

Florence is a private person, just the opposite of the guy she married. When cancer was diagnosed in April 2004, she never talked about it, never cried about how sick she was. Instead, she was always upbeat. A year later, she's still cooking and keeping up the house—won't even let me make my bed. Yes! I've been blessed!

Patricia Ann, "Patty," was our first-born, on Dec. 13, 1949. She was such a delightful child. We lived on North Street in Little Italy in very spartan surroundings, but we didn't notice. Old Sofia Rannelli next door used to beg us to let her babysit for Patty. She called the baby "Lee-la."

Our second child, Elizabeth, was born Sept. 12, 1953, when

we lived on Geranium Street. Betty never crawled as a baby. She sat on her butt and moved by moving her feet—hard to describe.

After the two adorable girls were born, we moved to Conway Street and we had a son, Anthony Francis, on Jan. 25, 1957. Every time we moved we had another kid. Florence says, please, no more moving.

Tony was always mischievous, just like other little boys. When he was six he announced he was going to run away from home. He packed his little suitcase, about the size of a telephone book, and off he went—next door to the Clausens. He was back in 10 minutes. I have it on film.

My children attended Saint Pascal's Elementary School and Hill-Murray High School before they went their separate ways for college.

Patricia went to Concordia and became an x-ray technician. She married William (Bill) Bloyer and had two children, Justin and Kirstin. She kept on balancing work and motherhood as supervisor of 30 x-ray technicians at Saint Paul Radiology. It was quite a responsibility and she eventually wanted to wind down. She went part-time and recently became certified as an MRI technician at Saint Paul Radiology, while she is also a CAT scan technician at Lakeview Hospital in Stillwater.

Patricia's son, Justin, is an airline pilot for American Eagle, a division of American Airlines. He has no interest in team sports such as baseball, basketball or football, but excels as a skier, skater and water skier. He is one of the premier players in an amateur hockey league. His wife is Dana Reis, a delightful, intelligent young lady. She is a manager at National Checking Company.

Patricia's daughter, Kirstin, is bright, beautiful and a graduate of the University of Minnesota. She has done extensive traveling throughout the world and is just starting on the path to her dream career, being a stockbroker.

Our son, Tony, is called that in the family, but professionally he is known as Anthony. He is a graduate of the University of Minnesota and received a law degree from William Mitchell

Our son, Tony, is a prosecutor for the city of Saint Paul.

College of Law in Saint Paul. He has a background in journalism, cable television, and promotion as well. After he got his law degree, he went to work for the Bureau of Criminal Apprehension before becoming a prosecuting attorney for the city of Saint Paul. He learned how to skate at age 45 and now plays in a senior men's hockey league.

It is the most devastating thing for me to talk about my dear daughter Elizabeth, who passed away in March 2001. It grieves me still.

CHAPTER 104

Elizabeth's Death

Eᴌɪᴢᴀʙᴇᴛʜ ᴡᴀꜱ ꜱᴜᴄʜ ᴀ ꜱᴡᴇᴇᴛ, ᴋɪɴᴅ, darling daughter—in her eyes, no one could do any wrong. She earned a bachelor's degree from the College of Saint Catherine, and studied at the University of Minnesota and at what is now the University of Saint Thomas.

She went to work for the city of Saint Paul in the Health Department, where she supervised the program called WIC (Women, Infants and Children), a supplemental government nutrition program. Ed Eberhardt, my friend and her supervisor at the Health Department, said Elizabeth was one of his most dedicated, intelligent employees with some of the best supervisory skills he had ever seen.

She rose to a position as budget analyst for the city of Saint Paul, but she found the work too stressful, and left to be a mail sorter with the U.S. Postal Service.

Our daughter Elizabeth was so kind that she believed no one could do any wrong.

234

In January 2001 Florence and I were vacationing in Arizona with Tony when we got a call from Patricia that Elizabeth was at United Hospital with a brain aneurysm.

We needed to come home immediately. The people at Northwest Airlines helped us change our tickets with as little fuss as possible, and we got home late the next morning, in time to see Elizabeth, who was already in the operating room.

As we walked down the hospital corridor, I could see Father Pingatore from Saint Ambrose and his assistant, Patricia Swanson. Only then did I realize the seriousness of the situation. Father Pingatore told me that Elizabeth had received the blessing of the sick, which from my youth I have known as "the last rites."

Elizabeth, her head already shaved for surgery, appeared quite solemn. She looked at me, smiled, and said, "Nunu." In Italian, it means "Dad." Those were her last words to me. I answered back, "Bobba Lou," which was her nickname.

After the surgery, she lived for 37 days without regaining consciousness. I never thought I would see the day I would pray for my daughter to die, but during those 37 days, I did just that.

It was the saddest time of my life. I can't explain the pain I felt—for days, months. Elizabeth was something special. And still is!!! Florence and I miss our daughter so much. Each day we talk about her. Everyone in the family loved her so very, very much.

When Elizabeth died, I made a pledge that I would go to church every day. More than four years later, I've missed a few days due to illness or inclement weather, but I've kept that pledge as best I could. I still feel sadness about my daughter's death, but I am able to experience joyful events that brighten my day.

CHAPTER 105

The Curtain Closes for Now

WHAT A FULL, JOYFUL LIFE the Lord has given me, full of adventure, friends, and most importantly, my family.

He gave me Florence, my devoted wife, three tremendous children, Patty, Elizabeth, Tony, who brought me joy, made me so proud of them. My grandchildren, Justin and his wife, Dana; Justin's sister, Kirstin, and Patty and her husband, Bill. And there was my sister, Mary, who was there for all of us, especially taking care of my papa, Antonio, and my mother, Aïda, and being attentive to Elizabeth while she was in a coma before her death.

In March 2005 I went into the Sun Ray library branch looking for the 1970 movie that gave me the reason to call my book *I Always Sang for My Father*. It was "I Never Sang for My Father" and starred Melvin Douglas and Gene Hackman. The movie wasn't available there, but the librarians made an effort and found a copy at another branch so I could see it again. I'm glad my dad wasn't a mean old cuss like the one Douglas portrayed.

Our household was a happy one. I can still hear my mother singing around the house. I can still see my dad coming home from playing bocce ball at the Yarussos' on a Sunday. Big smile on his face, a warm greeting—you could see he'd had a good day.

And brothers Nick and Al—we always looked out for each other. Nick and my childhood sweetheart, Alvira Corbo, died on the same day in July 2002. I went to Alvira's wake but I couldn't go to her funeral: It was at the very same time as Nick's.

Al died just a few months later, in December 2002. The day before he died, he and I went over to Turtle Lake, Wis., not to the casino but to visit a fellow musician, Jimmy Messicci, who in the 1950s used to play on WCCO-TV every day in the afternoon on the Jim Arlen Show.

Now, after both of them are gone, the three of us brothers were selected for the Minnesota Radio Hall of Fame in the fall of 2005. I represented the two of them at the ceremony and was proud and pleased to do it.

Another sad day was February 6, 2006. My favorite brother-in-law, Joe Valento, passed away. What a truly nice man he was. He was called "The Candy Man" because he always had candy on hand for children and adults. He was a bocce ball champion. I'm going to miss him so very much.

That first radio station we built together, the one in Stillwater, is still there. We made the call letters WSHB (which stood for "White Bear Lake, Stillwater, Hudson and Bayport"); then it was WAVN ("We accent valley news"), next WTCN ("Twin Cities News"), after that WEZU (in my opinion the best—"EZ listening for U") and then WMGT ("Mighty").

Any entertainer will tell you that one of the toughest parts of a performance is getting off the stage gracefully. So I'll just say, what a blessed life I have had. Thank you, Lord, and . . .

. . . good night, Elizabeth.

To order additional copies of *I Always Sang for My Father*

Web: www.itascabooks.com

Phone: 1-800-901-3480

Fax: Copy and fill out the form below with credit card information. Fax to 763-398-0198.

Mail: Copy and fill out the form below. Mail with check or credit card information to:

Syren Book Company
5120 Cedar Lake Road
Minneapolis, MN 55416

Order Form

Copies	Title / Author	Price	Totals
	I Always Sang for My Father / Vic Tedesco	$15.95	$
		Subtotal	$
		7% sales tax (MN only)	$
		Shipping and handling, first copy	$ 4.00
	Shipping and handling, ___ add'l copies @$1.00 ea.		$
		TOTAL TO REMIT	$

Payment Information:

__ Check Enclosed __ Visa/MasterCard		
Card number:	Expiration date:	
Name on card:		
Billing address:		
City:	State:	Zip:
Signature:	Date:	

Shipping Information:

__ Same as billing address __ Other (enter below)		
Name:		
Address:		
City:	State:	Zip: